AMERICAN
SOCIAL
MOVEMENTS

D0104987

D0109426

THE
ANTISLAVERY
MOVEMENT

Jodie Zdrok-Ptaszek, *Book Editor*

Daniel Leone, *President*

Bonnie Szumski, *Publisher*

Scott Barbour, *Managing Editor*

Stuart B. Miller, *Series Editor*

GREENHAVEN PRESS
SAN DIEGO, CALIFORNIA

THOMSON

GALE

Detroit • New York • San Diego • San Francisco
Boston • New Haven, Conn. • Waterville, Maine
London • Munich

Library of Congress Cataloging-in-Publication Data

The antislavery movement / Jodie Zdrok-Ptaszek, book editor.
    p. cm. — (American social movements series)
  Includes bibliographical references and index.
  ISBN 0-7377-1047-0 (pbk. : alk. paper) —
ISBN 0-7377-1048-9 (lib. : alk. paper)
    1. Antislavery movements—United States—History—Sources.
2. Slavery—United States—History—Sources. 3. Abolitionists—United States—History—Sources. I. Zdrok-Ptaszek, Jodie.
II. Series.

E449 .A623575 2002
326'.8'0973—dc21   2001050161

Cover photo: Library of Congress
North Wind Picture Archives, 98, 151, 171

Printed in the USA

CONTENTS

Chapter 1 • ORIGINS OF THE ANTISLAVERY MOVEMENT

> The concepts of freedom and individual rights were
> invoked in the Declaration of Independence and in
> the Constitution, yet the young nation possessed
> slaves. Some Americans were able to reconcile free-
> dom and slavery; others in the revolutionary era
> were troubled by the contradiction and voiced their
> opinion about the evils of enslavement.

> In the aftermath of the Revolution, a number of
> state and local antislavery societies were formed, and
> many of them partook in a national convention that
> met periodically from 1794 to 1829. By circulating
> petitions and public addresses, they hoped to per-
> suade people to recognize the evils and injustices of
> slavery.

> As more states entered the Union and slavery began
> to expand, members of the American Convention
> sought to implement a plan for emancipation. The
> convention argued that once freed, these former
> slaves should be educated and given land to cultivate
> for themselves.

Chapter 2 • A BURST OF REFORM: THE 1830s AND 1840s

Chapter 4 • ABOLITIONIST VOICES

FOREWORD

H istorians Gary T. Marx and Douglas McAdam define a
social movement as "organized efforts to promote or resist change in society that rely, at least in part, on noninstitu-
tionalized forms of political action." Examining American social movements broadens and vitalizes the study of history by
allowing students to observe the efforts of ordinary individuals and groups to oppose the established values of their era, often in unconventional ways. The civil rights movement of the
twentieth century, for example, began as an effort to challenge
legalized racial segregation and garner social and political rights
for African Americans. Several grassroots organizations—
groups of ordinary citizens committed to social activism—
came together to organize boycotts, sit-ins, voter registration
drives, and demonstrations to counteract racial discrimination.
Initially, the movement faced massive opposition from white
citizens, who had long been accustomed to the social standards
that required the separation of the races in almost all areas of
life. But the movement's consistent use of an innovative form
of protest—nonviolent direct action—eventually aroused the
public conscience, which in turn paved the way for major legislative victories such as the Civil Rights Act of 1964 and the
Voting Rights Act of 1965. Examining the civil rights movement reveals how ordinary people can use nonstandard political strategies to change society.

Investigating the style, tactics, personalities, and ideologies
of American social movements also encourages students to
learn about aspects of history and culture that may receive
scant attention in textbooks. As scholar Eric Foner notes,
American history "has been constructed not only in congressional debates and political treatises, but also on plantations and
picket lines, in parlors and bedrooms. Frederick Douglass, Eu-
gene V. Debs, and Margaret Sanger . . . are its architects as well
as Thomas Jefferson and Abraham Lincoln." While not all

American social movements garner popular support or lead to epoch-changing legislation, they each offer their own unique insight into a young democracy's political dialogue.

Each book in Greenhaven's American Social Movements series allows readers to follow the general progression of a particular social movement—examining its historical roots and beginnings in earlier chapters and relatively recent and contemporary information (or even the movement's demise) in later chapters. With the incorporation of both primary and secondary sources, as well as writings by both supporters and critics of the movement, each anthology provides an engaging panoramic view of its subject. Selections include a variety of readings, such as book excerpts, newspaper articles, speeches, manifestos, literary essays, interviews, and personal narratives. The editors of each volume aim to include the voices of movement leaders and participants as well as the opinions of historians, social analysts, and individuals who have been affected by the movement. This comprehensive approach gives students the opportunity to view these movements both as participants have experienced them and as historians and critics have interpreted them.

Every volume in the American Social Movements series includes an introductory essay that presents a broad historical overview of the movement in question. The annotated table of contents and comprehensive index help readers quickly locate material of interest. Each selection is preceded by an introductory paragraph that summarizes the article's content and provides historical context when necessary. Several other research aids are also present, including brief excerpts of supplementary material, a chronology of major events pertaining to the movement, and an accessible bibliography.

The Greenhaven Press American Social Movements series offers readers an informative introduction to some of the most fascinating groups and ideas in American history. The contents of each anthology provide a valuable resource for general readers as well as for enthusiasts of American political science, history, and culture.

Rewarded Reform: Morality and Persistence in the Antislavery Movement

O n the night of November 7, 1837, Elijah Parish Lovejoy was fatally shot five times. He died in the arms of a friend. Two days later, on his thirty-fifth birthday, he was buried in an unmarked grave.

Lovejoy was a Presbyterian minister and the founder of a religious newspaper, the *St. Louis Observer.* As editor, he took a stand against slavery in America. Lovejoy's strong condemnations aroused bitter resentment in Missouri, which entered the Union as a slave state. But the minister had witnessed much cruelty in his state, including a slave being burned at the stake. He felt it was his moral duty to speak out. After numerous protests against his editorials and the wrecking of his press by proslavery mobs, Lovejoy fled to Alton in the nonslaveholding, or free, state of Illinois. There he helped form the Illinois Anti-Slavery Society and continued to publish his antislavery views in the *Alton Observer.* Once again, though, residents were infuriated by Lovejoy's editorials. Due to its proximity to slaveholding states, Alton had many proslavery sympathizers. Within one year, mobs destroyed three of Lovejoy's presses and threw them into the Mississippi River.

Lovejoy remained persistent. One night he and twenty of his supporters went to a warehouse to guard his fourth press, which awaited installment at the *Observer.* A proslavery crowd formed outside the building. Soon a riot broke out and gunfire was exchanged. The mob set fire to the warehouse roof. As Lovejoy was trying to put out the fire, he was blasted with a double-barreled shotgun five times.

Elijah Lovejoy's murder roused antislavery sentiment in the free states of the North. To the abolitionists, Lovejoy was a martyr who died defending his right to free speech and press. To those who supported slavery, the abolitionist editor was rash and disrespectful. Slavery was condoned in many Southern states of the nation, and where the practice was outlawed in the North, proslavery advocates believed their rights as citizens were being trampled by a partisan government. One outraged commentator on Lovejoy's death even compared his murderers to the nation's forefathers who stood up to defend their liberty during the American Revolution.

Lovejoy's story, however, is a testament to the power and influence of the antislavery movement in America. The antislavery cause, or abolitionism, was one of the most effective social reform movements in the nation's history. What began as a moral argument against bondage quickly turned into a political movement and eventually pushed the nation into civil war. Complex, diverse, and infused with emotion, the antislavery movement ultimately touched every segment of American society and brought about changes that forever shaped the nation.

THE INSTITUTION OF SLAVERY

Slavery played a significant role in American history. It was not, however, an institution unique to the United States. Slavery can be traced back to many ancient civilizations. Its European roots reach back to the societies of Greece and Rome. Even after the fall of Rome in the fifth century, the empire's slavery system was eventually transformed into medieval serfdom. It remained in this modified form for many centuries. Bondage did not reappear in Europe until the fifteenth century. In 1442 Portuguese sailors brought back African slaves from the continent's west coast. The slaves were treated as an owner's property and could be used to do any menial chores that the owner desired. This business was profitable among the seafaring countries of

Europe and thus began the transatlantic African slave trade.

Over the next few hundred years, the need for slave labor grew. The European nations ventured across the Atlantic and began to colonize North America, the West Indies, and South America. Sugarcane, tobacco, and coffee plantations became an important economic factor in these colonies, and slaves were needed to work the land. Initially the colonists hoped to employ natives as slaves. However, many natives died from diseases brought from Europe; others avoided the oppressive labor through resistance or other means. Because they were far from familiar homelands and familiar faces, African slaves proved more docile. As a result, more and more Africans were brought over to work in the fields. Estimates as to the number of Africans deported into New World slavery between the fifteenth and nineteenth centuries range from 10 to 15 million.

SLAVERY IN AMERICA

There was no slavery in Virginia, the first American colony, when it was founded in 1607. It was not until 1619 that twenty Africans were sold to the settlers there. Even so, the slave trade did not flourish immediately. White indentured servants, bound to their masters for a certain amount of time, outnumbered black slaves for much of the seventeenth century. The indentured servants sold themselves into service, but only for a period of time, usually long enough to pay off the cost their masters had to pay to bring them to America. Toward the end of the century, fewer and fewer indentured migrants came from Europe. Africans, who were in service for life, were used in their place, and by the mid–eighteenth century slavery existed in all thirteen colonies.

Even when slavery existed in all of the colonies, differences between the North and the South became apparent. The Northern economy was based on small farms and on manufacturing. The slave population was comparatively small. The Southern economy was based on large agricultural plantations. Southern slaves had much bigger economic and social roles than their Northern counterparts. Simply put, slavery was much more important in the South, even before the colonies gained independence.

THE BEGINNINGS OF THE ANTISLAVERY SENTIMENT

The growth of bondage throughout the colonial era stirred moral concerns among at least one religious group, the Society of Friends from Pennsylvania. Also known as Quakers, the Society of Friends was the first organization to question the morality of slavery. It remained part of the antislavery movement throughout its duration. Believing slavery to be incompatible with Christianity, the Quakers condemned slaveholders in a 1758 Philadelphia meeting. Slave traders were excluded from membership in the Society of Friends in 1761, and within a decade, the Friends forbade slaveholding among their ranks as well.

The Quakers were instrumental in the creation of the first antislavery organization in America, the Pennsylvania Society for the Abolition of Slavery. It was formed in April 1775, the same month that the American Revolution began. Initially called the Society for the Relief of Free Negroes Unlawfully Held in Bondage, the abolitionist group expanded over the course of a few years and prompted the formation of antislavery societies in other cities. Over time, members of the Pennsylvania Society included such public figures as Benjamin Franklin, George Washington, Alexander Hamilton, and Thomas Paine.

ANTISLAVERY IN THE AFTERMATH OF THE REVOLUTION

When the Revolution began there were about a half million slaves in America. With the nation's quest for liberty and independence came questions about freedom and slavery. Each of the Northern states abolished slavery between 1774 and 1804. Some chose immediate emancipation, and others elected gradual emancipation. In the South, meanwhile, slavery expanded in the years after the Revolution. The agricultural society needed this manpower in order to survive, and the slave population doubled between the years 1770 and 1810. However, this is not to say that the morality of slavery was not questioned in the South during this period. Indeed it was, and some slave owners made private decisions to emancipate their slaves. Yet the overall bondage increased when the invention of the cotton gin (1793) opened up a huge new industry. Cotton production soon became the economic anchor of the South; the demand for labor rose, and more slaves were brought over from Africa. The delicate and uncomfortable questions surrounding freedom and slavery, however, did not subside. Indeed, the aftermath of the Revolution and the ideals of liberty it represented aroused antislavery feelings with slightly more conviction than during colonial times.

The principles of the new American government were set down in the Constitution. And since slavery was part of the nation, the framers of the Constitution had to deal with the issue from the outset. Although the word *slave* was not used in the final document, the institution of slavery was addressed indirectly by means of the "three-fifths clause." According to the Constitution, the citizen population of a state determined that state's representation in Congress and the Electoral College. Although slaves were not deemed citizens, the South felt entitled to some sort of extra representation. The compromise clause counted three-fifths of the slave population as a means of determining representation.

In addition to the three-fifths clause, the Constitution also included a fugitive slave clause that required the return of runaway slaves to their owners and prohibited a restriction on the slave trade for the next twenty-year period. Lastly, the Constitution allowed the federal government to suppress domestic rebellions of any sort, including slave insurrections. Such concessions were made with an eye closer to the present than the future. At the time the Constitution was being written, the founding fathers were concerned, above all, with establishing a Union. Some feared that without these concessions, the slave states might refuse to join.

EARLY NINETEENTH-CENTURY ACTION

The Union's first national antislavery society was formed in 1794. Called the American Convention, this society consisted of delegates from local and state antislavery societies. The organization met yearly from 1794 until 1829 and promoted gradual abolition in all states. In the early nineteenth century, however, the government had no incentive to upset the fragile alliance of states by taking measures to end slavery. As time went on, Northern antislavery sentiment increased, and pressure was put on the government to find an answer to the "peculiar institution." Coupled with internal pressure, foreign governments also tried to sway American politicians to abolish slavery. Although European traders had first opened the slave market, by the nineteenth century slavery ran counter to the ideals of "enlightened" governments of Europe. Finally, in 1807, Congress passed an Act to Prohibit the Importation of Slaves into the United States. Signed into law by President Thomas Jefferson, the act mandated the end of the slave trade by January 1, 1808. However, the last-minute influx of slaves before that legislation took effect, combined with the natural self-perpetuation among slaves, resulted in a sizable slave population in the South. By 1810 about 1.2 million slaves lived in the United States.

The issues of slavery, population, and representation arose repeatedly as new states entered the Union. Whether a state was "free" or "slave" affected the balance of power—and thus the way the slavery question was addressed—in Congress. As a result of the Missouri Compromise of 1820, an official dividing line (latitude 36°30') separated "free" from "slave" states.

Meanwhile, antislavery sentiment continued to build. In 1822 Denmark Vesey, himself a free black, was executed after his plot to organize a slave rebellion in South Carolina was uncovered. Further antislavery agitation occurred in 1829 when black abolitionist David Walker issued his *Appeal to the Colored Citizens of the World*. In the *Appeal,* Walker threatened insurrection if slavery were not abolished and if blacks were not granted equal rights. The South believed Northern antislavery

THE MISSOURI COMPROMISE OF 1820

Free states

Missouri Territory
(Free soil)
Missouri Compromise
1820

Arkansas Territory
(Slave soil)
Missouri Compromise
1820

Spanish
Mexico

Slave states

1000 Km
1000 Mi.

groups were inciting this type of violence and were in effect waging war on the Southern way of life.

THE ANTISLAVERY MOVEMENT COMES INTO ITS OWN

It was the decade of the 1830s, though, that witnessed a sudden flourish of abolitionist feeling. At this time, abolitionism transformed from a moderate movement into a militant crusade. Many antislavery proponents were not simply pushing for gradual abolition but demanding immediate emancipation.

From the 1830s to the 1850s, the United States experienced an "Age of Reform." Besides abolition, some of the reform movements that appeared included women's rights, temperance, prison reform, education reform, and an improvement of working-class conditions.

The growing influence of evangelical religion at this time was key to this atmosphere of reform. Religious revivals swept the North during the late 1820s and early 1830s, and charismatic preachers such as Charles Finney won over a number of converts. Future abolitionists such as Arthur and Lewis Tappan and Theodore D. Weld were among those to fall under Finney's sway and engage wholeheartedly in social reform as a result.

Although this spirit of reform is usually attributed to a renewal in religious and evangelical fervor, some reformers were motivated by secular, societal ideals rooted in the Enlightenment. Morality was the unifying force behind the diverse antislavery movement. Whether the inspiration was religion, secular ethics, or personal experience, the abolitionists decried the immorality of the institution of slavery. Historian Dwight L. Dumond offers insight into the abolitionist perspective. Beyond Scriptures and morality, the antislavery reformers condemned slavery because it ran contrary to fundamental principles in American life and, as Dumond writes,

> plundered the slaves of their inalienable rights as men: ownership of their own bodies: freedom of choice, as to use of time and occupation; the rights of marriage, family life . . . the right to worship . . . the right to cultivate their minds . . . the right to protect themselves, their homes, and their families against violence; the right to protection of the law. These were things which, especially in those days of rugged individualism, made a powerful impression on the average American.[1]

Those abolitionists who had more personal reasons for joining the movement were, typically, former slaves themselves. These men and women were often called on to give public accounts of their life in bondage and their escapes. Frederick Douglass, one of the most well known of these activists, wrote editorials for Northern newspapers and gave lectures at antislavery gatherings. Other former slaves, such as Harriet Tubman, were active members of the Underground Railroad that aided fugitive slaves in escaping the South. Although the reformers' cause was heroic, their challenge was great. In 1830 there were still 2 million slaves in the nation.

SPREADING THE WORD

In 1831 a slave rebellion in Virginia led by Nat Turner captured the nation's attention. That same year, William Lloyd

Garrison, one of the most fervent abolitionists in the history of the movement, launched the *Liberator*. This abolitionist newspaper from Massachusetts used incendiary language to condemn slavery and advocate immediate emancipation.

In 1832 Garrison founded the New England Anti-Slavery Society. Its members viewed slavery as contrary to the precepts of Christianity and sought to persuade others of the immorality of the institution. The success of the society and the growing number of abolitionist reformers prompted the creation, by Garrison and others who adopted his creed of nonviolent agitation, of a nationwide organization called the American Anti-Slavery Society.[2] This became the most well known and influential organization in the antislavery movement.

The abolitionists, in both national and local societies, spread their messages through a variety of means and types of propaganda, including newspapers, sermons, petitions to Congress, children's literature, slave narratives, and enthusiastic rallies. The antislavery novel *Uncle Tom's Cabin* by Harriet Beecher Stowe (daughter of evangelical preacher Lyman Beecher), published in 1851, remains one of the most well known examples of abolitionist propaganda.

The trend of newly formed antislavery societies continued throughout the 1830s, and by 1838 there existed about 1,300 societies with a total membership of 109,000. These statistics do not, however, reflect unity among abolitionists. On the contrary, the various degrees of antislavery zeal combined with differences in strategies often led to divisiveness. Even Douglass and Garrison, once close associates, grew apart when Douglass launched his own newspaper. The gap widened when Douglass declared himself a voting abolitionist, whereas Garrison objected to the morality and utility of activity in political parties. The two traded barbs via their newspapers. In 1853 Garrison, clearly frustrated, wrote, "The history of the Anti-Slavery struggle has been marked by instances of defection, alienation, apostasy, on the part of some of its most efficient supporters for a given time. . . . Mr. Douglass now stands unmasked . . . and as artful and unscrupulous a schismatic as has yet appeared in the abolition ranks."[3]

CHALLENGES TO THE MOVEMENT

One of the greatest challenges the abolitionists had to overcome was their minority status. They were, on the whole, small in number. To be successful, they were compelled to rely on zeal and not on numbers. In addition to small numbers, abolitionists had to overcome the obstacle, curiously enough, of their own activism. Abolitionists had a loud voice and were sometimes viewed as fanatics. Antislavery agitation was often met with public opposition, and abolitionist literature was even burned. Throughout the 1830s abolitionist meetings were invaded by angry mobs led by propertied men. Such mobs could easily get out of control, as in the case of Elijah Lovejoy.

Opposition to antislavery activities was not limited to the general public. Antislavery reformers made themselves heard, but politicians made *themselves* silent. The political indelicacies of the slavery issue continued to be a problem, and federal legislators preferred not to confront it. In 1836 a "gag rule" was passed in the House of Representatives. This gag rule was intended to suppress congressional debate on the slavery issue and banned consideration of antislavery petitions, with violators facing the threat of censure. That slavery had encountered a political stalemate did anything but diminish antislavery sentiment, despite the fact that the gag rule was not repealed until 1844.

Indeed, the propaganda surrounding the Underground Railroad was stepped up during this period. The "railroad" was a series of hiding places and safe houses that runaway slaves used as they fled north. White and black abolitionists alike helped fugitives escape to Canada or free states in a loosely organized system that was first termed *Underground Railroad* in print in the early 1840s. Between 1840 and 1860, about a thousand or so slaves a year escaped successfully as "passengers." Abolitionists made no secret of rescue attempts and successes. Much like the *Liberator,* the activities and accounts of the Underground Railroad served to illustrate the evils of slavery and the importance of liberating those in bondage.

ANTISLAVERY ON THE POLITICAL AGENDA

While Garrison and others worked outside the political arena, some abolitionists advocated direct political action. This was the basis for the Liberty Party, which was founded in 1840 and ran James G. Birney as a presidential candidate in 1840 and 1844. Although marginal at first, the Liberty Party evolved into the more inclusive Free Soil Party, which ran candidates in 1848 and 1852.

The emergence of antislavery political parties was also facilitated by events that put the slavery issue on top of the nation's agenda. By the late 1840s the United States had acquired an enormous amount of territory as a result of the Mexican War and the annexation of Texas. Once again, questions arose concerning the admittance of states as "free" or "slave." In response, Congress enacted the Compromise of 1850. In accordance with this legislation, California was admitted as a free state, and New Mexico and Utah were afforded popular sovereignty (the power of the state's residents to decide on their own whether to permit slavery). In addition, this legislation abolished the slave trade in Washington, D.C., and created a stricter Fugitive Slave Law that would penalize anyone interfering with the pursuit and capture of fugitive slaves. The latter component was no doubt in response to the successes of the Underground Railroad.

Popular sovereignty was tried again several years later when more states entered the Union. With the Kansas-Nebraska Act in 1854, the dividing line that had been set by the Missouri Compromise of 1820 was declared null and void. From then on, the citizens of new states entering the Union would decide whether to permit slavery within their borders. But allowing popular sovereignty to rule resulted in local skirmishes and bloodshed when people on both sides of the slavery question fought for their view to become law. And it is no coincidence that in 1854 a new political party—the Republican

Party—was born in protest to the extension of slavery in the western territories. The Republican Party represented largely Northern interests, and symbolized increasing sectional tensions and loyalties.

The division between the North and the South grew sharper and more violent as the 1850s continued. Historian Eric Foner writes that by the 1850s, "the antithesis between 'free society' and 'slave society' had coalesced into a comprehensive world view glorifying the North as the home of progress, opportunity, and freedom."[4] Of course, this resulted in the South being cast as the land of bondage. Several episodes served to exacerbate the tensions, not the least of which was the 1856 caning of a Republican senator from Massachusetts, Charles Sumner. In the course of his powerful antislavery speech "Crime Against Kansas," Sumner took aim at two proslavery Democratic senators, Stephen Douglas and Andrew Butler. Three days after the speech, Butler's nephew, Congressman Preston Brooks of South Carolina, entered the Senate chamber and beat Sumner unconscious with a cane. Sumner was unable to return to the Senate for three years because of his injuries, and in Northern eyes, the caning represented the brutality of the South. Brooks, meanwhile, was regarded as a defender of Southern honor and was reelected in the next election.

Also contributing to sectionalism was John Brown's failed but militant raid on a federal arsenal in Harpers Ferry, Virginia, in 1859. Brown was a vigilante who believed God had decreed that slavery should end in a violent cleansing of the South. Brown and several followers marched on the arsenal in hopes of arming nearby slaves and sparking a general revolt. Federal troops put an end to Brown's plan, and the aged zealot was later hanged for his crime. Not only did this incident compound sectional tension, but it also led to the ever-present question about method and strategy: How to go about attaining emancipation? The John Brown affair reminded many people of the Nat Turner revolt of 1831. One militant newspaper editor concluded, "Emancipation must take place, and soon. There can be no long delay in the choice of methods. If

John Brown's be not soon adopted by the free North, then Nat Turner's will be by the enslaved South."[5] The threats of violent interference antagonized the South, which assumed that the growing antislavery sentiment in the North would eventually sweep through the government and bring about the use of federal troops to quash slavery.

These fears seemed to manifest in 1860. That year, Abraham Lincoln was elected president. Lincoln was a Republican who opposed the expansion of slavery but did not advocate abolition. Regardless, the Southern states could not tolerate the shift in political control and, believing that the existence of slavery was threatened by an antislavery government, they seceded from the Union. The sectional struggle had entered a dramatic, violent stage, and 4 million slaves awaited an uncertain future.

CIVIL WAR AND EMANCIPATION

The fate of the antislavery movement was decided by the Civil War (1861–1865). Although the war was initially conducted to restore the Union, emancipation became a war aim as a result of the Emancipation Proclamation. Issued in 1862 and put into effect in 1863, Lincoln's Emancipation Proclamation freed slaves in the seceded states. As a military order, the proclamation had no legal effect. Emancipation became constitutionally legal only with the ratification of the Thirteenth Amendment in 1865, when the Union was fully restored. As for Lincoln's role and eventual commitment to emancipation, Foner states that "for Lincoln, the war's deepest meaning lay in the 'new birth of freedom' occasioned by the abolition of slavery. . . . The Union's triumph consolidated the northern understanding of freedom as the national norm. In the process, the meaning of freedom, and the identity of those entitled to enjoy its blessings, were themselves transformed."[6]

Once the goal of abolition was attained and slaves were emancipated at the end of the Civil War, many reformers channeled their energies into further assisting the black community. Although the end of slavery was indeed a tremendous victory, emancipation brought with it a number of new social questions. The Reconstruction era in the South was a divisive period. There were conflicting goals as the different political and social elements were drawn together in the postwar Union. For the emancipated slaves, called freedmen, concerns arose about education, economic independence, and political participation. Those mostly likely to help them voice these concerns were usually former abolitionists.

Abraham Lincoln

Racial prejudice proved to be a significant stumbling block to the abolitionist movement. During the nineteenth century many people did not view blacks and whites as equals in society. A number of whites could not envision themselves living alongside blacks, and this attitude posed difficulties for reformers advocating emancipation and integration. Indeed, this remained an obstacle long after the abolitionists attained their goal of emancipation.

The abolitionists achieved their purpose despite encountering disagreement in their own ranks. As in most social movements, the antislavery reformers were individuals whose zealousness differed by degree. They were a diverse group of people who approached the slavery question with a variety of ideas, experiences, and motivations. Above all, they were not unified in their strategies. Some, for example, preferred propaganda tactics, others dared to help slaves escape, and still others insisted that nothing short of war would end slavery. The antislavery fire risked consuming itself on more than one occasion but remained strong enough to affect national policy. When the Civil War ended in 1865 and the Thirteenth Amendment was ratified, William Lloyd Garrison stated,

> As it respects the abolition of slavery, we are no longer peculiar. Once we stood and were obliged to stand alone, and

represented about all the abolition sentiment there was in the land; now the millions of people who have voted on this question, and the States that have registered their verdict for the abolition of slavery and the amendment of the Constitution, have changed the position of this nation from darkness to light, and from the rule of slavery to the triumph of liberty.[7]

THE PEOPLE BEHIND THE MOVEMENT

A reform movement is directed by the people behind it. The abolitionists were ordinary citizens, both men and women, black and white, who viewed slavery as an injustice and remained steadfast in their position even as the country plunged into political chaos.

The antislavery movement seeped into every facet of society by the time of the Civil War. It was an emotional movement that either attracted or repelled people, but it did not allow them to be indifferent. Motivated by morality, the antislavery reformers communicated the justice of their cause to the rest of the nation. Their persistence was well rewarded.

NOTES

1. Quoted in Hugh Hawkins, ed., *The Abolitionists: Means, Ends, and Motivations,* 2nd ed. Lexington, MA: D.C. Heath, 1972, pp. 39–40.

2. The American Anti-Slavery Society split in 1840 when disputes arose concerning women's rights. Garrison and others sought to make this one of the society's causes; others disagreed. Garrison remained in the society until it dissolved in 1870. Arthur and Lewis Tappan formed the American and Foreign Anti-Slavery Society, which focused only on ending slavery. Both societies were successful agitators for the antislavery cause.

3. Quoted in Benjamin Quarles, ed., *Great Lives Observed: Frederick Douglass.* Englewood, NJ: Prentice-Hall, 1968, p. 108.

4. Eric Foner, *The Story of American Freedom.* New York: W.W. Norton, 1998, p. 91.

5. Quoted in Benjamin Quarles, ed., *Blacks on John Brown.* Urbana: University of Illinois Press, 1972, p. 38.

6. Foner, *The Story of American Freedom,* p. 97.

7. Quoted in Hawkins, *The Abolitionists,* p. 224.

ORIGINS OF THE ANTISLAVERY MOVEMENT

AMERICAN
SOCIAL
MOVEMENTS

Slavery and Freedom in the Revolutionary Era

Eric Foner

Eric Foner is a professor of American history and has authored a number of major works in that field. In *The Story of American Freedom*, he traces the concept of freedom as it has evolved throughout America's history. This selection provides an overview of American pro- and antislavery sentiment during the last decades of the eighteenth century. The piece also addresses the meaning given to "freedom" in the revolutionary era. During the nation's bid for independence, the institution of slavery in a land espousing freedom was justifiable to some people but troublesome to others. Even after the Revolution, the hard-won ideals of the new United States did not yet bring a resolution to this contradiction.

The contradiction between freedom and slavery is so self-evident that it is difficult today to appreciate the power of the obstacles to abolition. At the time of the Revolution, slavery was already an old institution in America; it existed in every state and formed the basis of the economy and social structure from Maryland southward. It was slavery that made the staple-producing colonies the richest region in British America. Already, as a French visitor observed, "command of a few negroes" was essential to the self-definition, the social standing, of southern planters. Thomas Jefferson, as is well known, owned over one hundred slaves at the time he wrote the immortal lines affirming the inalienable right to liberty, and everything he cherished in his own manner of life, from lavish entertainments to the leisure that made possible the pursuit of arts and sciences, ultimately rested on slave labor.

CONTRADICTIONS IN THE RIGHT TO LIBERTY

Slavery for blacks did not necessarily contradict white Americans' understanding of freedom. It could in fact be argued that slavery made republican freedom possible, for by eliminating the great bulk of the dependent poor from the political nation, it left the public arena to men of propertied independence. For many Americans, owning slaves offered a route to the economic autonomy widely deemed indispensable to genuine freedom (a point driven home by a 1780 Virginia law that rewarded veterans of the War for Independence with three hundred acres of land—and a slave). The republican vision of a society of independent men actively pursuing the public good could easily be reconciled with slavery for those outside the circle of citizenship. In a republic, [British economist] Adam Smith pointed out, it would be all the more difficult to abolish slavery since "the persons who make all the laws in that country are persons who have slaves themselves"—thus, the "freedom of the free" helped to produce "the great oppression of the slaves." So, too, the liberal definition of freedom as essentially private and of the political community as a group of individuals seeking protection for their natural rights could readily be invoked to defend bondage. Nothing was more essential to liberal freedom than the right of self-government and protection of property against interference by the state. These principles suggested that it would be an infringement of liberty to relieve a man of his property (including slave property) without his consent. The right to property, Virginian Arthur Lee insisted, was "the guardian of every other right, and to deprive a people of this, is in fact to deprive them of their liberty." If government by the consent of the governed was the essence of political freedom, then to require owners to give up their slave property would reduce *them* to slavery.

Nonetheless, by imparting so absolute a value to liberty,

sweeping away forms of partial freedom so prevalent in the colonial era, and positing freedom as a universal entitlement rather than a set of rights specific to a particular place or people, the Revolution inevitably raised questions about the status of chattel slavery in America. Before independence, the nation's first chief justice, John Jay, later remarked, "very few ... doubted the propriety and rectitude" of slavery, even though enlightened opinion in the Atlantic world (exemplified, for example, in the writings of Montesquieu, David Hume, and Adam Smith) had come to view slavery as morally wrong and economically inefficient, the relic of a barbarous past. During the revolutionary era, slavery for the first time became a focus of public debate in America. It was not a British critic but the Pennsylvania patriot Benjamin Rush who in 1773 called upon "advocates for American liberty" to "espouse the cause of ... general liberty," and warned that slavery was one of those "national crimes" that one day would bring "national punishment." In the following year, Massachusetts clergyman John Allen lamented that Americans were making a "mockery" of their professed love of liberty "by trampling on the sacred natural rights and privileges of the *Africans.*" Not all these comments emanated from the North, where slavery was far less powerfully entrenched than in the plantation regions of Maryland, Virginia, the Carolinas, and Georgia. Jefferson, at least in private, strongly condemned chattel slavery as a system "one hour of which is fraught with more misery, than ages of that which [the colonists] rose in rebellion to oppose."

EXTENDING THE RHETORIC OF THE REVOLUTION

The Revolution inspired widespread hopes that slavery could be removed from American life. Most dramatically, slaves themselves appreciated that by defining freedom as a universal right, the revolutionists had devised a rhetoric that could be deployed against chattel bondage. The language of liberty echoed in slave communities, North and South. Living amid freedom but denied its substance, slaves appropriated the patriotic ideology for their own purposes. The first concrete steps toward emancipation were "freedom petitions"—arguments for manumission presented to New England's courts and legislatures in the early 1770s by enslaved African-Americans. Once the War for Independence began, the British offered freedom to slaves who joined the royal cause. Nearly one hundred thousand, including one-quarter of all the slaves in South Carolina, deserted their owners (although not a few were subsequently reenslaved in the West Indies). George Washington himself saw seventeen of his slaves flee to British lines. Thousands more escaped bondage by enlisting in the Revolutionary Army.

Blacks recognized both hypocrisy and opportunity in the ideology of freedom. The most insistent advocates of freedom as a universal entitlement were African-Americans, who demanded that the leaders of the struggle for independence live up to their professed creed, thus extending the concept of liberty into unintended realms. As early as 1766, white Charlestonians had been shocked when their opposition to the Stamp Act under the slogan, "Liberty and stamp'd paper," inspired a group of blacks to parade about the city crying "Liberty." Nine years later, the Provincial Congress of South Carolina felt compelled to investigate the "high notions of liberty" the struggle against Britain had inspired among the slaves.

In 1776, the year of American independence, Lemuel Haynes, a black member of the Massachusetts militia and later a celebrated minister, urged that Americans "extend" their conception of freedom. If liberty were truly "an innate principle" for all mankind, Haynes insisted, "even an African [had] as equally good a right to his liberty in common with Englishmen." Throughout the revolutionary period, petitions, pamphlets, and sermons by blacks expressed "astonishment" that white patriots failed to realize that "every principle from which America has acted" demanded emancipation. Blacks sought to alter the language of politics, insisting that the nation understand slavery as a concrete, brutal reality, not an abstract condition or metaphor. Petitioning for their freedom in 1773, a group of New England slaves exclaimed: "We have no property! We have no wives! No children! We have no city! No country!" For blacks, slavery meant the denial of all the essential attributes of freedom, not merely the loss of personal autonomy or lack of political self-determination.

Most slaves of the revolutionary era were only one or two generations removed from Africa. They did not need the ideology of the Revolution to persuade them that freedom was a birthright; the experience of their parents and grandparents suggested as much. . . . Blacks insisted that the slave, not the master, genuinely craved liberty. "My love of freedom," wrote the black poet Phillis Wheatley in 1783, arose from the "cruel fate" of being "snatch'd from Afric's" shore. Yet, if traditional African societies knew the desire not to be a slave, the modern idea of freedom was born in the West. In the world from which the slaves had been forcibly removed, where individuals existed within a wide network of communal and kin relationships and social identity depended on being anchored in a web of power and authority, personal freedom was an oxymoron. By invoking the Revolution's ideology of liberty to demand their own rights and defining freedom as a universal entitlement, blacks demonstrated how American they had become, even as they sought to redefine what American freedom in fact represented.

For a brief moment, the "contagion of liberty" appeared to threaten the continued existence of slavery. During the 1780s, a considerable number of southern slaveholders, especially in Virginia and Maryland, voluntarily emancipated their slaves. Farther south, however, the abolition process never got underway. In the North, every state from New Hampshire to Pennsylvania took steps toward emancipation, the first time in recorded history that legislative power had been invoked to eradicate slavery. But even here, where slavery was peripheral to the economy, the slowness of abolition reflected how powerfully the sanctity of property rights impeded emancipation. Generally, abolition laws provided for the liberty of any child henceforth born to a slave mother, but only after he or she had served the mother's master until adulthood as compensation for the owner's future loss of property rights.

At the Constitutional Convention of 1787, as Madison recorded, "the institution of slavery and its implications formed the line of discrimination" in many debates. The fifty-five men who gathered in Philadelphia to draft the document included numerous slaveholders, as well as some dedicated abolitionists. Madison, who, like Jefferson, was a Virginia slaveholder who despised slavery, told the convention that the "distinction of color" had become the basis for "the most oppressive dominion ever exercised by man over man." Yet later, Madison assured delegates to the Virginia ratifying convention that the Constitution offered slavery "better security than any that now exists." And so it did. For the Constitution prohibited Congress from abolishing the African slave trade for two decades; required states to return to their owners fugitives from bondage; and provided that three-fifths of the slave population be counted in determining each state's representation in the House of Representatives and its electoral votes for president. To be sure, the words "slave" and "slavery" did not appear in the original Constitution—a concession to the sensibilities of delegates who feared they would "contaminate the glorious fabric of American liberty." As Luther Martin, a Maryland attorney who opposed ratification, wrote, his fellow delegates "anxiously sought to avoid the admission of expressions which might be odious to the ears of Americans." But, he continued, they were "willing to admit into their system those *things* which the *expressions signified.*"

Clearly, the Constitution's slavery clauses were compromises, efforts to find a middle ground between the institution's critics and defenders. Taken together, however, they managed to strengthen the institution of slavery and leave it more deeply embedded in American life and politics. The slave trade clause allowed a commerce condemned by civilized society, and which had been suspended during the War for Independence, to continue until 1808. Partly to replace slaves who had escaped to the British, and partly to provide labor for the expansion of cotton production into the upcountry, South Carolina and Georgia took advantage of the twenty-year hiatus before the trade's abolition to import some ninety thousand additional

Africans, about one-quarter of all the slaves brought to British North America after 1700. The fugitive slave clause accorded slave laws "extraterritoriality," that is, the condition of bondage adhered to a person even after he or she had escaped to a jurisdiction where slavery had been abolished. John Jay, while serving in Madrid on a diplomatic mission, once wrote of how he missed the "free air" of America. Jay was probably unaware of the phrase's ironic implications, for in the *Somerset* case of 1772, the lawyer for a West Indian slave brought to Britain had obtained his client's freedom by invoking the memorable words, "the air of England is too pure for a slave to breathe." Yet in the United States, the Constitution's fugitive slave clause made all the states, including those that had abolished slavery, complicitous in maintaining the institution's stability. For slaves, there was no "free air" in America.

The federal structure, moreover, insulated slavery in the states from outside interference, while the three-fifths clause allowed the white South, and especially the planter class, to exercise far greater power in national affairs than the size of its free population warranted. Partly as a result, of the first sixteen presidential elections, between 1788 and 1848, all but four placed a southern slaveholder in the White House. Even the initial failure to include a Bill of Rights resulted, in part, from the fact that, as South Carolina delegate Charles Cotesworth Pinckney explained, "such bills generally begin with declaring that all men are by nature born free," a declaration that would come "with a very bad grace, when a large part of our property consists in men who are actually born slaves."

THE REVOLUTION'S CONTRADICTORY IMPACT

All in all, the Revolution had a contradictory impact on American slavery and, therefore, on American freedom. Gradual as it was, the abolition of slavery in the North drew a geographical line across the new nation, creating the portentous division between free and slave states. Abolition in the North, voluntary emancipation in the Upper South, and the escape of thousands from bondage created, for the first time in American history, a sizable free black population (not a few of whose members took new family names like Freeman or Freeland). On the eve of independence, virtually every black person in America had been a slave. Now, a free community, with its own churches, schools, and leadership class, came into existence, constituting a standing challenge to the logic of slavery, a haven for fugitives, and a springboard for further efforts at abolition.

For many Americans, white as well as black, the existence of slavery would henceforth be recognized as a standing affront to the ideal of American freedom, a "disgrace to a free government," as a group of New Yorkers put it. In 1792, when Samuel Jennings of Philadelphia painted *Liberty Displaying the Arts and Sciences,* he included among the symbols of freedom a slave's broken chain, graphically illustrating how freedom had become identified not simply with political independence but with emancipation. Certainly, after the Revolution it would be difficult to employ slavery as a metaphor without triggering thoughts about actual slaves. Nonetheless, the stark fact is that the Revolution did not rid American society of slavery. Indeed, thanks to the natural increase of the slave population, soon to be supplemented by a reopened slave trade, there were considerably more slaves at the end of the revolutionary era than at the beginning. The first national census, in 1790, revealed that the half-million slave population of 1776 had grown to some 700,000.

Throughout the Atlantic world, the upheavals of the age of revolution posed a threat to slavery. In 1794, the French Convention proclaimed abolition (only to see slavery restored by Napoleon a few years later). Emancipation was a goal of the leaders of independent Haiti and nearly all the Latin American liberators. Only in the United States did the creation of a new nation-state strengthen the institution. The British poet Oliver Goldsmith might well have been speaking of the revolutionary generation when he commented on mankind's propensity "to call it freedom, when themselves are free."

The Need to Abolish Slavery

AMERICAN CONVENTION OF
DELEGATES FROM ABOLITION SOCIETIES

The American Convention of Delegates from Abolition Societies was the primary national organization from 1794 to 1829 to promote the abolition of slavery. Composed of local and state antislavery societies, the delegates held twenty-four conventions over the thirty-three-year period. Until 1821, the main goal of each convention was to improve the condition of slaves and to protect slaves that were free. The following piece is taken from the minutes of the first convention in January 1794. The intentions of the organization, mainly to circulate petitions and to write addresses to the American people, are expressed in the minutes. In the address "to the Citizens of the United States," the Convention explains its reasons for promoting antislavery, the inconsistency of slavery with principles of freedom, and the notion that slavery violates divine precepts.

In Convention of Delegates, from the Societies established, in different parts of the United States, for promoting the abolition of slavery, assembled at the City Hall, in the city of Philadelphia, January 1, 1794. . . .

INTENTIONS

First, That a memorial be presented to Congress, praying that Body to prohibit, by law, the citizens of the United States, from carrying on a commerce, in slaves, for the supply of foreign nations; and, also, to prohibit foreigners from fitting their ships in the ports of the United States, for the purpose of carrying on the slave-trade.

Excerpted from the minutes and address from the First Convention of the American Convention of Delegates from Abolition Societies, January 1, 1794, Philadelphia.

Second, That memorials and petitions be presented to the Legislatures of such of the states as have not yet passed laws to prohibit the importation of slaves—to enact laws for that purpose; and, also, to the Legislatures of the individual states—to prevent slaves from being forcibly carried away; and to grant to such of them as have been, or may be emancipated, such a participation in civil privileges, as, by the diffusion of knowledge among them, they may, from time to time, be qualified to enjoy.

Third, That addresses be sent to the different Abolition Societies, recommending to them to continue their zeal and exertions, in behalf of such of our African brethren as are yet in bondage; also, to use their utmost endeavours to have the children of the free and other Africans, instructed in common literature—in the principles of virtue and religion, and afterwards in useful mechanical arts; thereby to prepare them for becoming good citizens of the United States.

Fourth, That an address be written, and published to the citizens of the United States, to impress upon them, in the most forcible manner, the obligations of justice, humanity and benevolence towards our African brethren, whether in bondage or free, and to request their concurrence with us in all the objects of the present Convention.

Fifth, That it be recommended to the different Abolition Societies, to appoint Delegates to meet in Convention, at Philadelphia, on the first Wednesday of January, 1795, and on the same day, in every year afterwards, until the great objects of their original association be accomplished....

OPENING COMMENTS

The address of the Delegates from the several Societies, formed in different parts of the United States, for promoting the abolition of slavery, in Convention assembled at Philadelphia, on the first day of January, 1794.

Friends and Fellow-citizens,

United to you by the ties of citizenship, and partakers with you of the blessings of a free government, we take the liberty of addressing you upon a subject, highly interesting to the credit and prosperity of the United States.

It is the glory of our country to have originated a system of opposition to the commerce in that part of our fellow-creatures, who compose the nations of Africa.

Much has been done by the citizens of some of the states to abolish this disgraceful traffic, and to improve the condition of those unhappy people, whom the ignorance, or the avarice of our ancestors had bequeathed to us as slaves; but the evil still continues, and our country is yet disgraced by laws and practices, which level the creature man with a part of the brute creation.

REASONS FOR ABOLITION

Many reasons concur in persuading us to abolish domestic slavery in our country.

It is inconsistent with the safety of the liberties of the United States.

Freedom and slavery cannot long exist together. An unlimited power over the time, labour, and posterity of our fellow-creatures, necessarily unfits men for discharging the public and private duties of citizens of a republic.

It is inconsistent with sound policy; in exposing the states which permit it, to all those evils which insurrections, and the most resentful war have introduced into one of the richest islands in the West-Indies.

It is unfriendly to the present exertions of the inhabitants of Europe, in favour of liberty. What people will advocate freedom, with a zeal proportioned to its blessings, while they view the purest republic in the world tolerating in its bosom a body of slaves?

In vain has the tyranny of kings been rejected, while we permit in our country a domestic despotism, which involves, in its nature, most of the vices and miseries that we have endeavoured to avoid.

It is degrading to our rank as men in the scale of being. Let us use our reason and social affections for the purposes for which they were given, or cease to boast a preeminence over animals, that are unpolluted with our crimes.

DIVINE JUSTICE

But higher motives to justice and humanity towards our fellow-creatures remain yet to be mentioned.

Domestic slavery is repugnant to the principles of Christianity. It prostrates every benevolent and just principle of action in the human heart. It is rebellion against the authority of a common FATHER. It is a practical denial of the extent and efficacy of the death of a common SAVIOUR. It is an usurpation of the prerogative of the GREAT SOVEREIGN of the universe, who has solemnly claimed an exclusive property in the souls of men.

But if this view of the enormity of the evil of domestic slavery should not affect us, there is one consideration more which ought to alarm and impress us, especially at the present juncture.

It is a violation of a divine precept of universal justice, which has, in no instance, escaped with impunity.

The crimes of nations, as well as of individuals, are often designated in their punishments; and we conceive it to be no forced construction, of some of the calamities which now distress or impend our country, to believe that they are the measure of evils, which we have meted to others.

The ravages committed upon many of our fellow-citizens by the Indians, and the depredations upon the liberty and commerce of others of the citizens of the United States by the Algerines [Algerian pirates], both unite in proclaiming to us, in the most forcible language, "to loose the bands of wickedness, to break every yoke, to undo heavy burthens, and to let the oppressed go free."

We shall conclude this address by recommending to you,

First, To refrain immediately from that species of rapine and murder which has improperly been softened with the name of the African trade. It is Indian cruelty, and Algerine piracy, in another form.

Secondly, To form Societies, in every state, for the purpose of promoting the abolition of the slave-trade, of domestic slavery, the relief of persons unlawfully held in bondage, and for the improvement of the condition of Africans, and their descendants amongst us.

The Societies, which we represent, have beheld, with triumph, the success of their exertions, in many instances, in favour of their African brethren; and, in a full reliance upon the continuance of divine support and direction, they humbly hope, their labours will never cease, while there exists a single slave in the United States.

A Plan for Emancipation

AMERICAN CONVENTION FOR
PROMOTING THE ABOLITION OF SLAVERY

The 1801 constitution of the American Convention of Delegates from Abolition Societies changed the organization's name to the American Convention for Promoting the Abolition of Slavery and Improving the Condition of the African Race. By 1821, with the Missouri Compromise and the expansion of slavery in view, emancipation and the education of slaves became the goals of the organization. The excerpt that follows is from the "plan" adopted by the Convention on October 3, 1821, for freeing slaves. Denouncing the rights denied to Africans and the evils of slavery, the American Convention plan proposes gradual but general and universal emancipation. The organization insists that such a plan would be neither new nor radical and points to slave emancipation elsewhere in the world as an example.

> *"We hold these truths to be self-evident, that all men are created equal; that they are endowed by their Creator with certain unalienable rights; among these are life, liberty, and the pursuit of happiness; that to secure these rights, governments were instituted, deriving their just powers from the consent of the governed."*

—Declaration of Independence

These self-evident truths, thus solemnly promulgated, and always admitted in theory, at least in relation to ourselves, are well-known to be partially denied or disregarded in most sections of the union, in relation to the descendants, of the African race. That a nation professing the principles of equal

Excerpted from the minutes of the Seventeenth Convention of the American Convention for Promoting the Abolition of Slavery and Improving the Condition for the African Race, October 3, 1821, Philadelphia.

rights, and loudly proclaiming the justice of its laws, should contain a population, amounting to nearly one-seventh of the whole, who know little of the operation of those laws, except as instruments of oppression, is one of those political phenomena, which prove how little the patriot's boast, or the orator's declamation is guided by the light of truth.

It must be admitted that it would neither be politic nor safe, for the present system of slavery in the United States to be long continued, without providing some wise and certain means of eventual emancipation.

Slavery with its present degrading characteristics, is a state of actual hostility between master and slave, in which "a revolution of the wheel of fortune, an exchange of situation, is among possible events; and this may become probable by supernatural interference! The Almighty has no attribute which can take part with us in such a contest."—Thomas Jefferson

SLAVERY'S EVILS

It is a truth generally acknowledged, that Slavery is an evil, not only by those whom principle, or education have taught to proscribe the practice, but by men of reflection, even in the very vortex of slavery. To condemn then, what few, if any, will presume to defend, is rendered unnecessary; and the ingenuity of the philanthropist would be more judiciously exercised in devising a practicable remedy for this deep-rooted disease, than in heaping reproaches upon those, who, by the conduct of their ancestors, are placed in the condition of masters of slaves. Few of those who from their childhood, have been placed in situations far removed from the scenes which slavery exhibits, can fully appreciate the difficulties, the vexations, and the anxieties, incident to the life of a slaveholder. To devise a plan, then, by which the condition, both of the master and slave may be meliorated, is a desideratum in the policy of this country:—A plan which will promote the immediate interest of the master, in the same ratio, that the slave is made to rise in the scale of moral and intellectual improvement; and which will eventuate in the ultimate enfranchisement of the long injured and degraded descendants of Africa. The evils of slavery being generally acknowledged, and its impolicy fully evinced, the important question which remains to be solved, will naturally present itself: What are the means by which this evil is to be removed, consistently with the safety of the master, and the happiness of the slave? Perhaps to some, this question, considered on the ground of absolute justice, may appear of easy solution: *Immediate, universal emancipation.*

But however pleasing the prospect may be to the philanthropist, of getting clear of one of the evils of slavery, yet a full examination of local circumstances, must convince us that this would be, to cut, rather than untie the Gordian knot.

A PLAN

Reformation on a large scale, is commonly slow. Habits long established, are not easily and suddenly changed. But were it possible to induce the inhabitants of the slaveholding states to proclaim liberty to the captives, and to let loose at once the whole tide of black population, it may reasonably be questioned whether such a measure would not produce as much evil as it would cure. Besides, such a measure, if it were practicable, would fall short of simple justice. We owe to that injured race, an immense debt, which the liberation of their bodies alone would not liquidate. It has been the policy of the slaveholder to keep the man whom he has doomed to interminable servitude, in the lowest state of mental degradation: to withhold from him as much as possible the means of improving the talents which nature has given him. In short, to reduce him as near to the condition of a machine as a rational being could be. Every inducement—every excitement, to the exertion and development of native talent and genius, is wanting in the slave.—Hence; to throw such a being, thus degraded, thus brutalized, upon society, and then expect him to exercise those rights, which are the birthright of every son and daughter of Adam, with advantage to himself, or to the community upon which he is thrown, is to suppose that the laws established for the government of universal nature, should in this case be changed. As well might we expect a man to be born in the full maturity of his mental faculties, or an infant to run before it had learned the use of its limbs.

A plan, then, for universal emancipation, to be practicable, must be gradual. The slave must be made to pass through a state or pupilage and minority, to fit him for the enjoyment and exercise of rational liberty.

"If then the extremes of emancipation, and perpetual, unlimited slavery be dangerous," and impolitic, "the safe and advisable measure must be between them."

GENERAL AND UNIVERSAL EMANCIPATION

And this brings us again the question, How can we get clear of the evils of slavery, with safety to the master, and advantage to the slave? For the solution of this difficult problem, the following outlines of a plan for a gradual, but *general* and *universal* emancipation is proposed. Let the slaves be attached to the soil,—give them an interest in the land they cultivate. Place them in the same situation in relation to their masters, as the peasantry of Russia, in relation to their landlords. Let wise and salutary laws be enacted, in the several slave holding states, for their general government. These laws should provide for the means of extending to the children of every slave, the benefits of school learning. The practice of arbitrary punishment for the most trivial offences, should be abolished.

An important step towards the accomplishment of this plan, would be, to prohibit by law the migration, or transportation of slaves from one state to another:—and also to provide, that no slave should be sold, out of the county, or town in which his master resides, without his own consent. Provision should then be made for the introduction of a system of general instruction on each farm or plantation; each slave who has a family should be furnished with a hut, and a portion of land to cultivate for his own use; for which he should pay to the landlord an annual rent. For each day he was employed by the master or landlord, he should be allowed a stipulated price: out of the proceeds of his stipulated wages, those things necessary for his comfortable maintenance, should be deducted, if furnished by the master.

The time given him to cultivate his allotment of ground, should be deducted from his annual hire. A wise and equitable system of laws, adapted to the condition of blacks, should be established for their government. Then a character would be formed among them; acts of diligence and fidelity would meet their appropriate reward, and negligence and crime would be followed by their merited chastisement. The execution of this plan, in its fullest extent, would be followed by increased profits to the landholder.

It would be productive of incalculable advantage to the slave, both in his civil, and moral condition:—And thus the interest of the master, and the melioration of the condition of the slave, would be gradually and reciprocally advanced in the progress of this experiment. Although legislative provisions would greatly facilitate the adoption of this plan, it is not necessary for individuals to wait the movement of government. Any one may introduce it on his own plantation, and reap many of its most important advantages.

NOT A NEW PLAN

The plan now proposed is not new. It is not a Utopian and visionary theory, unsupported by experience. It has been successfully tried in the Island of Barbadoes, by the late Joshua Steele; and the result exceeded his most sanguine expectations. "The first principles of his plan," says Dr. Dickson, "are the plain ones, of treating the slaves as human creatures: moving them to action by the hope of reward, as well as the fear of punishment: giving them out of their own labours, wages and land, sufficient to afford them the plainest necessaries:—And protecting them against the capricious violence, too often of ignorant, unthinking, or unprincipled, and perhaps drunken men and boys, invested with arbitrary powers, as their managers, and 'drivers.' His plan is founded in nature, and has nothing in it of rash innovation. It does not hurry forward a new order of things;—it recommends no fine projects, or ticklish

experiments; but, by a few safe and easy steps, and a few simple applications of English law, opens the way for the gradual
introduction of a better system." "To advance above three
hundred debased field Negroes, who had never before moved
without the whip, to a state nearly resembling that of contented, honest and industrious servants; and, after paying them
for their labour, to triple, in a few years, the annual net clear-
ance of his estates—these were great achievements, for an aged
man, in an untried field of improvement, preoccupied by in-
veterate vulgar prejudices. He has indeed accomplished all that
was really doubtful or difficult in the undertaking; and perhaps
all that is at present desirable, either to owner or slave. For he
has ascertained as a fact, what was before only known to the
learned as a theory, and to practical men as a paradox:—that
the paying of slaves for their labour, does actually produce a
very great profit to their owners."

Antislavery in the Early Nineteenth Century

Merton L. Dillon

Merton L. Dillon, a retired professor of history at Ohio State University, is a specialist on the history of slavery and the author of several books on abolitionism. In the following excerpt, taken from *The Abolitionists: The Growth of a Dissenting Minority,* Dillon examines the antislavery movement as it developed in the early nineteenth century. Dillon points out that despite a growing belief that slavery was wrong, most Americans still possessed deep racial prejudice. Abolitionists, therefore, had a daunting task before them. Not only did they have to demonstrate the evils of the institution, but also they had to show white America that slaves were intelligent and talented and deserved equal treatment as citizens of the nation. Furthermore, while abolitionists tried to give a voice to this struggle, politicians found it politically beneficial to remain silent, thus ensuring the nation would not come to any collective decision on the issue of slavery.

W ith the rapid spread of cotton production across the lower South after 1800, slavery attained still more widespread economic importance than before, and fewer voices were raised against it. Instances of antislavery success became infrequent, even while abolitionist rhetoric grew more intense. Antislavery appeals in the North aroused diminishing response, and in the South, antislavery sentiment was in fast retreat.

Rhode Island abolitionists observed as early as 1806 that members of what they called "the young and rising generation" felt less repugnance against slavery than did older men who had lived through the inspiring days of the American Revolution. Apparently the same was true in the South. At one time Jefferson had put his trust for eventual antislavery action in young men whose ideas were formed during the Revolutionary period, but he lived long enough to become as disappointed in the new generation as he was in his own. When in 1814 his youthful and idealistic neighbor Edward Coles disclosed to him his hopes that slavery could be destroyed, Jefferson responded with the amazing statement that "your solitary but welcome voice is the first which has brought this sound to my ears."

THE COLONIZATION MOVEMENT

A stumbling block to antislavery action appeared everywhere in the form of racial prejudice. Proposals for abolition were always countered with questions about what would be done with the supposedly inferior and dangerous Blacks after emancipation. Few indeed could accept as anything less than madness proposals to incorporate them into American society on terms of equality. Instead it was generally taken for granted that freed slaves ought to be sent to Africa or otherwise removed from close contact with Whites.

In 1816, a group of reformers who sought the end of slavery as a great evil—but who at the same time rejected as a similar evil the prospect of the Blacks' remaining in America—formed the American Colonization Society. Its program of transporting free Blacks to Africa, although from one point of view a drastic solution to the problems of slavery and racial adjustment, may be regarded as conservative because it made no effort whatever to alter the racial prejudices of white Americans, accepting these as unchangeable.

The 1820s was the heyday of the colonization movement, the decade when it won endorsement from an array of prominent clergymen and of such influential statesmen as Henry Clay. But backing by great personages proved insufficient to accomplish the Society's purpose. The success of its ambitious plan required a degree of organizational effort and financial support that only the national government could supply. Such a large undertaking, even if it were otherwise feasible, ran so counter to the decentralizing tendencies of the time that it could not be adopted. Southerners would never agree that slavery and racial problems came within the sphere of federal power. Furthermore, most free Blacks resisted the prospect of removal to Africa, though there were conspicuous exceptions; a number of Blacks at this time, as in every subsequent generation, viewed their prospects in white America as hopeless and accordingly sought some form of separation.

Despite the inability of the Colonization Society to carry out its program, it did succeed in spreading information about slavery and the oppression of free Blacks into communities where these matters were not objects of daily observation. In that respect the work of the American Colonization Society may be regarded as a constructive prelude to the widespread abolitionist campaigns of the 1830s. But it had a negative effect as well, for by incessantly emphasizing the degradation of free Blacks, it probably strengthened the hold of racial prejudice on the minds of white Americans. On that account alone, most abolitionists came to regard the American Colonization Society as working against their own program and against the welfare of the Blacks.

HELPING TO REMOVE PREJUDICE

Clearly unable to reverse the economic and social forces that so powerfully supported the growth of slavery, the early abolitionists believed they could at least help to remove racial bias, one of slavery's strongest buttresses. Accordingly, they devoted much of their effort before 1830 to extending humanitarian aid to the black population that already constituted a conspicuous minority in nearly every Northern city. The ending of slavery in the North had not been accompanied by change in the racial attitudes that for so long had supported it. If anything, prejudice increased as the numbers of free Blacks grew and as the insecurities resulting from rapid economic and social change were felt throughout white society.

Prejudice was not expressed in verbal slurs and social slights alone. Far more serious was the fact that custom barred most Blacks from economic and educational opportunity. Although striking examples can be cited of Blacks who overcame all such obstacles, the majority were shut out by prejudice from sharing in the profits and advantages of the growing American economy.

Abolitionists resolved to change that situation. A prerequisite to emancipation and to the elevation of free Blacks, so they believed, was the elimination of racial prejudice. Blacks must be recognized as men and brothers. If they were proved to be the equals of other Americans in capacity and accomplishment, abolitionists reasoned, the only justification for enslavement and discrimination would disappear. Accordingly, as early as 1800, abolitionists expanded their program to embrace educating free Negroes and otherwise helping them to rise above the lowly position most of them then occupied. Such endeavor would satisfy the obligations of philanthropy—always a prime consideration for Quakers and other religious reformers—but its more significant function would be to demonstrate the abilities of Negroes and thereby prove current racial practices unwarranted. With the walls of prejudice shattered, reasonable men would stop scorning Blacks and begin to treat them in every respect as equals. Slavery itself, it was thought, could not long withstand that development. It should be noted that the reformers who held such expectations hoped to eliminate prejudice among Whites by working with Blacks. They would "improve" and "elevate" the Negro until he reached a level Whites found acceptable.

In order to make a start toward those goals, several early abolition societies—including some in the Upper South—founded schools for free Negroes and tried to find employment for black youths. The abolitionists' schools supplemented instruction that Blacks already supplied for themselves under the guidance of the Negro churches and mutual benefit societies that emerged in black communities at the end of the eighteenth century.

Abolitionists launched their educational efforts with all the energy that optimism can lend to a cause, yet none of the experiments succeeded to the degree their backers had anticipated. Neither black children nor abolitionists were responsible for the failure. Abolitionists' schools provided ample evidence, if more were needed, of the Negro's intellectual capacity. According to numerous reports, black children learned to read and to compute about as well as white children; their accomplishments in craftsmanship were commendable. Yet none of those attainments helped very much to elevate Blacks in the eyes of the white majority.

PREJUDICE REMAINS

Racial prejudice proved stronger and more stubborn than abolitionists had realized. Although many white persons learned of the achievements of Blacks both in schools and outside of them, they seldom allowed such knowledge to alter their bias. The effect of that stubborn prejudice on black children was often discouragement. The sunny predictions that education opened the door to opportunity were false. When black children came to understand this fact, their eagerness for such training was likely to diminish. The Negro's successes in education confirmed the optimism of philanthropists but did little to alter the majority's racial views. All available evidence suggests that despite the efforts of white humanitarians and of Negroes themselves, racial restrictions and discriminations increased rather than diminished after 1820.

In the all-important area of achieving recognition of racial equality, the early abolitionists for the most part failed. But in the political arena they achieved occasional success. Their most conspicuous legislative accomplishment—after passage of gradual emancipation laws in the North—was the decision of Congress in March 1807 to end the foreign slave trade, a measure supported by American statesmen, including President Jefferson, as well as by little-known antislavery reformers. In the same month that Congress outlawed the African trade, the English Parliament passed a similar law. Those victories, important though they were thought to be, were in a sense hardly more than symbolic, for while they significantly limited the African slave trade, the prohibition was but imperfectly enforced and still left the extensive domestic slave trade undisturbed. Further, enactment of the laws had the effect of causing some reformers to relax their antislavery efforts for a time because they believed that the end of the African trade had put slavery itself on the way to extinction. In a sense, those optimists were not mistaken, for a long debate preceding the measure's passage brought into the open for the first time the cruelties inherent in slavery and in that way stimulated a humanitarian controversy over the institution that not even the most determined opposition could ever quite still.

POLITICAL DEFEATS AND TRIUMPHS

Antislavery failures were more frequent than successes after 1800, however, and probably more important in their consequence. One of the earliest of these defeats, and the one that most severely shocked abolitionists, was the refusal of Congress in 1820 to halt the admission of Missouri as a slave state. Even though later abolitionists would interpret the exclusion of slavery from the rest of the Louisiana Purchase north of 36°30' as a major achievement, in 1820 they viewed the restriction as trivial compensation for the fact that slavery had been allowed to expand into new regions. "Hell is about to enlarge her borders and tyranny her domain," was the despairing comment of the Quaker abolitionist editor Elihu Embree, when he received the news.

The Missouri Compromise convinced opponents of slavery that they could not depend on Providence to achieve their goals for them but that they must themselves act forcefully in the antislavery cause. An opportunity to test their strength and resolution soon appeared on the northwestern frontier of the American settlement. In 1823, in the infant state of Illinois, carved from the Northwest Territory from which slavery supposedly had been forever excluded by the Ordinance of 1787, ambitious settlers of Southern origin laid plans to call a state constitutional convention whose members, they hoped, could find a way to legalize slavery.

A full-scale antislavery movement was soon underway in Illinois as preachers, editors, and politicians combined forces to persuade the electorate to vote down the proposed convention. From his office in Tennessee, Benjamin Lundy, the Quaker editor of the *Genius of Universal Emancipation,* sent antislavery arguments to Friends in Illinois as ammunition in the campaign. From Philadelphia, Quaker humanitarians, including the illustrious Nicholas Biddle, who as president of the Second Bank of the United States would a few years later gain notoriety as an object of Andrew Jackson's wrath, supplied the antislavery forces with money and pamphlets. In Illinois itself, John Mason Peck, a Baptist preacher, traveled up and down the state organizing church members and clergymen against the proposal. Presiding over the entire coalition was the Virginia-born associate of Jefferson, Governor Edward Coles, who a few years earlier had freed his slaves and moved to Illinois.

The outcome of the political campaign was one of the few antislavery triumphs of the decade, as aroused voters soundly defeated the convention proposal at the polls. The victory over pro-slavery forces in Illinois had been achieved by using the safe and prudent means early abolitionists believed would be sufficient to end slavery everywhere—peaceful, rational persuasion and conventional political action. But the victory could not be repeated. Never again would such moderate means suffice to defeat the proponents of slavery, because at no other point of conflict were antislavery forces ever more than a minority. That fact in part accounts for the growing frustration of abolitionists and for their willingness by 1830 to abandon their earlier expectations and to adopt more extreme goals and tactics than those advocated by eighteenth-century antislavery partisans. The situation that confronted them must now be examined if the extent of their problem is to be understood.

The dominant political fact in the United States by 1830 was the creation of the Jacksonian party, democratically based and singularly attentive to pro-Southern, pro-slavery interests.

The new party's implication for the abolitionist cause was ominous, for Jacksonian democracy represented, among other things, obedience to popular will. In the South, popular will generally supported slavery; in the North, it tolerated the debasement of the free Negro. For those reasons, the growth of political democracy damaged the antislavery cause rather than aided it.

Although Jacksonian leaders disagreed on numerous issues of public policy, they could unite behind the determination to maintain silence on slavery and thereby, in effect, to safeguard it. In many parts of the North the rise of the Jacksonians brought to office men whose ties with the South were intimate and whose prospects for continued political success depended on retaining the approval of Southern party leaders. And a few years later, the Whig party, developed in opposition to Jackson, also often looked to Southern votes to help carry its candidates to office. Neither party dared sacrifice support by taking antislavery stands or even by tolerating them. A tacit agreement among party leaders kept slavery out of politics. Public discussion of slavery, politicians understood, would tend to weaken the institution of slavery itself as well as disrupt party structure. An antislavery political policy would assure the loss of Southern votes and risk Northern votes too. For while Northerners held practically no slaves, the North's involvement with slavery was only slightly less complete than that of the South.

NORTHERN INVOLVEMENT

Northern involvement was primarily economic. Much of the profit of Northern business derived from Southern trade and hence ultimately from slavery. This tie grew ever closer. Powerful Northeastern interests—especially shipping, textile manufacturing, and the cotton trade—flourished because of their Southern connections. Much the same thing was true in border areas of the new Northwestern states, where businessmen soon developed lucrative trade relations with the South. The economic welfare of the entire nation, in a sense, became tied to slavery. The bulk of American foreign exports consisted of slave-grown cotton. From its sale abroad came those credits that supported American purchases in Europe. Hence, American imports of manufactured goods and American international finance likewise heavily depended, in the final analysis, on slavery.

For those reasons, the abolitionists' program to destroy slavery appeared to run counter to progress and to the national interest. With some justice, abolitionists might even be considered subversive or "un-American," for by 1830 the United States had become a great slaveholding republic. Only an American blind to the events of his day could fail to see that American social and economic development was taking place with slavery at its base and that the nation's future growth apparently was pledged to its continuance.

Further, quite apart from their economic interest in slavery, a majority of Northerners were as intent as any Southerner to maintain white supremacy. Slavery kept most Negroes securely in the South. Its abolition presumably would leave them free to move to the North, a prospect that much of the Northern population dreaded. The dictum of the influential historian of the South, Ulrich B. Phillips, that the central theme of Southern history was the determination to keep the South a white man's country might, with accuracy, be recast to read: "A central theme of *American* history was the determination to keep the *United States* a white man's country." Slavery and its corollary of white supremacy were thoroughly enmeshed with American political and economic institutions. Abolition, it appeared, could not be accomplished without unparalleled disruption of the entire social order.

The problem facing abolitionists thus was staggering. The problem was not, as Stanley Elkins has suggested, that the United States lacked institutions through which slavery might have been ameliorated or abolished but rather that most of the institutions it did have were heavily involved with slavery. The ending of slavery would require such a vast reconstruction of the American system as to constitute revolution. Few aspiring businessmen and few clergymen in the national denominations—whose membership was in large part Southern—could support abolition. No politician whose election depended on more than a small, homogeneous constituency dared advocate such a program or even allow it to be advanced within his district.

LOSING THE CONTEST?

By any index that might be applied, abolitionists appeared to be losing the contest with slavery. Slavery was a stronger, more widespread institution in 1830 than it had been ten years earlier. Its spread into the Southwest continued unimpeded as cotton production increased. The domestic slave trade flourished, bringing renewed prosperity to the Upper South, where cotton and the plantation system had little hold. The influence of slaveholding states in determining national policy had in no way declined. Northern prejudice against free Negroes had not lessened, and sympathy for abolitionist programs had not appreciably increased. Economic interest and racial bias had moved the nation still further from the Revolutionary ideals upon which abolitionists believed it had been formed. Politicians and patriots continued to assert attachment to the noble and venerable ideals of liberty, equality, and opportunity, but the words uttered so easily in Fourth of July orations only partially corresponded to American reality.

Early nineteenth-century reformers—among whom abolitionists were only one group among several—seized every opportunity to warn against what they regarded as a dangerous decline in the nation's moral standard. Intensely religious persons in particular detected from certain recent changes in popular outlook and emphasis evidence of American degradation. A decline in the influence of clergymen and churches accompanied the new, all-absorbing popular interest in secular politics. Growing materialism, loss of spiritual values, and neglect of the ideals enunciated in such documents as the Declaration of Independence, seemed to some persons to constitute an emergency which called for the utmost in exertion if the nation were to avoid destruction. A deepening anxiety was experienced in certain ecclesiastical and political circles, especially those of New England and New York, as they watched control of the nation falling into the hands of Western and Southern interests who neither accepted Northeastern leadership nor shared Northeastern values. To such Easterners, the nation appeared to be in the grip of forces oblivious to any principle transcending the acquisition of wealth and power. America was losing its spiritual purity in an all but universal grasping for material advantage.

A BURST OF REFORM: THE 1830S AND 1840S

Abolitionism and the Age of Reform

LOUIS FILLER

Louis Filler is a professor emeritus of American Civilization from Antioch College. In addition to being a professional historian and author, he is also an editor and lexicographer. In the following selection, Filler summarizes antislavery in the Age of Reform, the period between 1830 and 1860. During this period of history, antislavery sentiments were being stirred by a variety of spokespeople including newspapermen and religious leaders. By 1840 abolition societies claimed hundreds of thousands of members, but it was clear that most resided in northern states that had already banned slavery. The animosity that grew between the free states and slaveholding states would eventually lead to war. But until then, Filler notes, the antislavery movement prospered and claimed small victories over the next twenty years.

The 1830–1860 era of reform was the most momentous of all eras since the Revolution, and not solely because it stirred the nation to deeds and asseverations which brought on civil war. It also raised fundamental questions respecting the nature of our civilization. Americans had always been, as a nation, partial to reforms simply because they were constantly disturbed by western movements and new influxes of population. They were thus subject to fluidity and change. A wide open frontier and an eager people unleashed from constrictive European circumstances made for a seething, anticipating society: one receptive to reform and also to counter-demands for law and order.

There were probably as many reformers during the pre-

Excerpted from *Abolition and Social Justice in the Era of Reform* edited by Louis Filler (New York: Harper & Row, 1972). Copyright © 1972 by Louis Filler. Reprinted with permission of HarperCollins Publishers, Inc.

ceding decade as during the 1830s, yet the later time was one of turmoil and challenge not found earlier. The problem which faced contemporaries of the reform era was to determine which factors had created the difference. . . .

AN AGE OF REFORMS

The antislavery crusade preempted public concern in the 1830s, but it was far from being the only issue to seize attention. The 1830s and beyond were a time of ferment in every human field, from prisons to the proper rearing of children. Public unrest raised momentous questions for religion and, indeed, created a host of human experiments which agitated the church establishments at every turn. Without such stirrings and attendant eloquence, it is difficult to see how, in a nation of sweat and labor, of contracts and traditions which chained its citizens to duties and obligations, slave labor could have become the moral issue which abolitionists proposed.

William Jay, who possessed a great name which he gave to the abolitionist cause, nevertheless feared the spiritual unrest which accompanied it. He feared its effects on morals and religion. Whether experiments in cooperative living, the proliferation of "free love" colonies and the emergence of new religious sects and ideas—including Mormonism, spiritualism and perfectionism—loosened the fabric of society was a question which the future would inherit. But the moral earnestness of the major leaders of reform and the incomparable eloquence of their spokesmen were factors which helped determine the course of reform and maintain them as a challenge to posterity. . . .

GARRISON AS A MORAL REFORMER

[For example] William Lloyd Garrison began his career not as an abolitionist but as a journalist and temperance advocate. Raised in a broken home and brother of a drunken seaman, Garrison saw in temperance a cause of primary social significance warranting his best talents. It also expressed his need for a simple, certain way of life, one of Christian rectitude. The moral assurance Garrison required could no more be satisfied by church ritual than it could satisfy Ralph Waldo Emerson, born in a family of ministers and graduate of the Divinity School of Harvard College. Emerson resigned his pastorate at the Second Church of Boston, where he was deemed popular and effective, because he could no longer sincerely administer the Lord's Supper. He needed a new faith, which introspection, travel and new associations matured. His invocations to nature, to self-reliance, to *oversoul* produced a minor scandal and contributed to a major social impulse toward self-expression at the expense of social forms. Garrison, too, in an era of individualists, had a career in journalism open to him which he put aside for more urgent matters. . . .

Garrison was made notorious by two equally undistinguished events. One was the 1829 Boston publication of David Walker's violent denunciation of white America, which furnished in the South a pretext for setting new curbs on the education and free movement of slaves. In August of 1831, an uprising of some seventy slaves in one of the southernmost counties of Virginia was led by Nat Turner, a brooding and religious Negro who had pondered the Bible and interpreted signs. The insurrectionary effort resulted in local atrocities on both sides and bared Virginia as a thoroughly frightened and concerned state. A momentous debate in its legislature on the issue of freeing or removing the Negroes from Virginia resulted in the total victory of the proslavery forces: the forces of simple suppression.

Although [Garrison's abolitionist newspaper] the *Liberator* attracted few readers, it circulated to editors everywhere, and its "incendiary" character was angrily noted in the southern press. It proceeded to make Garrison a symbol of all the things it feared the North capable of tolerating. In passionately demanding Garrison's suppression, it stirred the feelings of numerous men and women in the free states. Some of these were roused to actions which quickly made abolition a major public issue.

Abolitionists were of every type and concern. They included John Greenleaf Whittier, born of humble people in Massachusetts and William Jay of New York, son of the late Chief Justice of the United States John Jay. The abolitionists included Lydia Maria Child, who, as a young woman, had made a name as a story-teller and composer of juvenilia and other welcome literary fare. Garrison drew her and her husband David Lee Child, a promising lawyer and editor, out of their respectable orbits and into antislavery work. Mrs. Child's *An Appeal in Favor of That Class of Americans Called Africans* (1833) narrowed her circle of friends but influenced such vital personalities as the eloquent Wendell Phillips and the rising "scholar in politics," Charles Sumner....

Thus, some abolitionists followed the lead of Garrison, who demanded that slavery be regarded as sinful and slaveholders as steeped in sin. Others held ... to greater or lesser degree that slavery was an unfortunate condition which afflicted the country and was to be expunged by a majority of the nation's voters. All abolitionists, however, were surrounded by religious imperatives which drove them, sometimes reluctantly, to nonconformist thought. Abolitionism was outstandingly ... a religiously-motivated development.

This drive toward a more vital church produced a host of extraordinary talents. One of the most remarkable in the 1830s was Theodore Dwight Weld, a young man of inspiring mien and eloquence, who began with temperance and a plan for building "manual labor" schools combining religious fervor with the discipline of work....

Later ... Weld became a vital force in the new American Anti-Slavery Society founded in Philadelphia in 1833. He organized the famous "Seventy": evangelical abolitionist agents whom he sent out to stir up the countryside. In 1839 he issued, under title of *American Slavery as It Is,* a powerful collection of items, mostly culled from southern sources, revealing the darker workings of the slavery system. It aggravated the feelings of thousands of otherwise neutral northern citizens and directly influenced writings by Harriet Beecher Stowe and Charles Dickens.

THE BRITISH CONNECTION

Thus abolition flourished in the North during the 1830s, while it withered in the South, foretelling a different career from that which the British were experiencing. They, too, had raised crusaders to fight the foreign slave trade and had put it outside the law—but there were no slaves in the British Isles. There the struggle was between Parliamentary factions free to deal as they pleased with their Caribbean islands, containing three-quarters of a million slaves. In London humanitarian debate on the slave trade practically foredoomed legal slavery. In the United States the states-rights compact permitted southern leaders to stand tall and thereby destroyed the middle ground of compromise which helped the British to ease their way through an awkward tangle of social and economic interests.

Between 1832 and 1838 Parliamentary rhetoric and petitions brought about the legal emancipation of slaves in the British islands at the resounding price of 20 million pounds. Abolitionists in America made every effort to impress this example upon their countrymen, with relatively little result. Whether British emancipation was successful or unsuccessful, and in what sense, remained unresolved in American debates. Whether it was or was not "at the expense" of the suffering British poor was an open question. Abolitionists sought British support and financial aid. They raised the patriotic ire of Democrats and slaveholders who read malice and meddling in American affairs into such donations and who profited from domestic memories of the two wars the nation had fought to be free of British influence.

AGITATION

Meanwhile, the years 1834 and 1835 were the abolitionists' time in America for sensational organization in the face of angry agitation. Riots punctuated their meetings, and the lives of abolitionists were threatened. In New York Lewis Tappan's home was gutted by mobsters. In Boston on a lurid occasion Garrison was led through the streets with the rope encircling him entering into legend as a prelude to his hanging. Birney escaped a Cincinnati mob by mere accident. And so with others. In 1837 Reverend Elijah P. Lovejoy died by gunfire at Alton, Illinois, defending his fourth press from determined anti-abolitionists who had already done away with three others. The next year in Philadelphia, Pennsylvania Hall, built by reformers to be a center for their friends and activities, was burned to the ground during dedication ceremonies.

The eternal question was whether these and other heroics dragged the nation forward toward emancipation in spite of itself or interfered with a slower, sounder growth of abolitionist sentiment, and, instead, created an angry, divided nation. That was the force of Birney's critique of Garrison. The question haunted reform activities throughout the decade. By its end many abolitionists, who had originally acknowledged Garrison's demand for an "immediatist" approach, were ready to repudiate his "aberrations." They repudiated his sweeping condemnation of the church as a proslavery institution. They saw no virtue in his condemnation of the government and the Constitution as instruments of evil. They wrote off as intolerable his millenarian acceptance of "universal reform" as disruptive of their abolitionist cause. This last tenet of Garrisonianism took its most acute form in the sect's approval of women's participation on the most active levels of abolitionism. Garrisonians believed that women merited places not merely in audiences or even merely prior places at Anti-Slavery Fairs but also on platforms and in policymaking committees.

The turmoil caused by Garrisonian agitation involved a vast spectrum of experimental personalities, entirely in the North, including Margaret Fuller, raised by her father to be a prodigy of learning, Abby Kelley, taken from the schoolroom to add spirit and eloquence to antislavery meetings and Maria Weston Chapman, of wealthy upbringing. The key sensation of the decade, so far as women's participation in public issues went, was provided by two carefully raised young women from one of the most distinguished of South Carolina families, Sarah and Angelina Grimké. . . .

Pious and searching, the young women joined the Philadelphia Quakers and were caught up in abolitionist talk and enterprises. Angelina, the younger and more vibrant of the two, in 1836 published her epochal *Appeal to the Christian Women of the South,* causing a scandal below the Mason-Dixon line and a sensation farther north. Soon, the Grimkés, determined to testify against slavery, offered semipublic addresses in churches under abolitionist auspices. The unprecedented nature of their exposure—as distinguished from that of "Fanny Wright" women and men—even under controlled conditions, drew them into the Garrisonian orbit. More conservative abolitionists feared the Grimkés might not only disgrace themselves but their cause. . . .

ACTIVISM AND ACCOMPLISHMENT

By 1838 the North seethed with abolitionist societies to some 250,000 in number and with many more friends and sympathizers. They divided roughly into sections. In New England Garrisonians generally dominated. They ranged from Nathaniel P. Rogers of New Hampshire, editor of the *Herald of Freedom,* whom even Garrison could not control, to Henry C. Wright, who persuaded Garrison to initiate a succession of radical innovations. The New York abolitionists sought to colonize New England with a more decorous group of abolitionists who would be less antagonistic to churches and less interested in women's participation. The moderates sent men of substance north, including Henry B. Stanton, one of the "Lane rebels" and husband of Elizabeth Cady Stanton, later a leader of the suffragists. Their movement failed. New Englanders, far removed from slavery, preferred to divide into evangelical abolitionists and skeptics.

New York and Pennsylvania activists tended to be more practical in their approach, if only because they were opposed by more powerful and varied interests. New York merchants, for example, had a heavy stake in the southern economy, and a greater number of Negroes resided among them than could be found farther north. Ohio had perhaps the best-balanced antislavery enterprise, drawing dedicated extremists of the stamp of John Brown of the Western Reserve and Salmon P. Chase of Cincinnati, who was reluctant to be termed an abolitionist at all. He clung to the Democratic party, but his actions in behalf of runaway slaves earned him the gratitude of the Negro community.

The abolitionists accomplished much during the 1830s. They won the right to free speech and press, and revealed southern inability to defend either. They raised the issue of slavery in the District of Columbia. Their persistent scrutiny of Texas developments ensured that it might make one slave state but not more than one. Their visits to Great Britain created a strong and informed auxiliary there.

More important, abolitionists multiplied their aid to runaways and raised constitutional questions respecting slave catching in free states which pierced to American democratic expectations. Since laws undermining slave rights might eat at the civil defences of whites (there were recorded cases of *white* persons seized and transported into slavery), partisans could elicit sympathy for Personal Liberty laws which impeded the work of professional slavers. Such laws created bonds between abolitionists and others in free states, including even antiabolitionists.

A major hero of what became known as the "underground railroad" was Thomas Garrett (1789–1871) of Delaware, a slave state strategically lying between slave Maryland and free Pennsylvania and New Jersey. In some thirty years of underground work this fearless Quaker was said to have aided more than 2,700 fugitive slaves to freedom. Numerous others beside Garrett risked prison, reputation and life itself to aid individual Negroes and to deny the sanctity of slave property. They also created indispensable liaison relations with Negro communities which sought without pause to help their own.

Yet all these victories excited still greater ambitions to advance antislavery beyond individuals and the subversion of laws helpful to the slavery system. Political abolition could gain no foothold in the 1830s, but moderates were increasingly determined to silence the troublesome Garrisonians. Differences reached a head in their Society's 1840 annual meeting in New York where Garrisonians pressed for women on committees. The antifeminist wing, outmaneuvered, left to set up the rival American and Foreign Anti-Slavery Society. Thus abolitionism entered the 1840s with two organizations claiming to represent it. A third political group moved to advance beyond the appeals of moderates or extremists.

Declaration of Sentiments of the American Anti-Slavery Society

WILLIAM LLOYD GARRISON

William Lloyd Garrison (1805–1879) is one of the antislavery movement's most famous leaders. He is noted as the founder and editor
of the *Liberator,* an abolitionist newspaper in press from 1831 to
1865. In December 1833, Garrison and over sixty other delegates,
black and white, men and women, met in Philadelphia to found the
American Anti-Slavery Society. From this meeting came the "Declaration of Sentiments," written by Garrison, the society's corre-
sponding secretary. As the platform of the society, this document
states the society's purpose and the goals it hoped to achieve. The
Declaration denounces slavery as a sin, calls for immediate emancipation, advocates nonviolence in pursuit of the war on slavery, and
condemns racism in all parts of society.

The Convention assembled in the city of Philadelphia, to
organize a National Anti-Slavery Society, promptly seize
the opportunity to promulgate the following Declaration of
Sentiments, as cherished by them in relation to the enslavement of one-sixth portion of the American people.

More than fifty-seven years have elapsed, since a band of patriots convened in this place, to devise measures for the deliverance of this country from a foreign yoke. The corner-stone
upon which they founded the Temple of Freedom was broadly
this—"that all men are created equal; that they are endowed by

Excerpted from "Declaration of Sentiments of the American Anti-Slavery Society," by
William Lloyd Garrison, *The Abolitionists: A Collection of Their Writings,* edited by Louis
Ruchames (New York: G.P. Putnam's Sons, 1963). Copyright © 1963 by Louis Ruchames.
Reprinted with permission of Penguin Putnam Inc.

their Creator with certain inalienable rights; that among these are life, LIBERTY, and the pursuit of happiness." At the sound of their trumpet-call, three millions of people rose up as from the sleep of death, and rushed to the strife of blood; deeming it more glorious to die instantly as freemen, than desirable to live one hour as slaves. They were few in number—poor in resources; but the honest conviction that Truth, Justice and Right were on their side, made them invincible.

REASONS FOR MEETING

We have met together for the achievement of an enterprise, without which that of our fathers is incomplete; and which, for its magnitude, solemnity, and probable results upon the destiny of the world, as far transcends theirs as moral truth does physical force.

In purity of motive, in earnestness of zeal, in decision of purpose, in intrepidity of action, in steadfastness of faith, in sincerity of spirit, we would not be inferior to them.

Their principles led them to wage war against their oppressors, and to spill human blood like water, in order to be free. Ours forbid the doing of evil that good may come, and lead us to reject, and to entreat the oppressed to reject, the use of all carnal weapons for deliverance from bondage; relying solely upon those which are spiritual, and mighty through God to the pulling down of strong holds.

Their measures were physical resistance—the marshalling in arms—the hostile array—the mortal encounter. Ours shall be such only as the opposition of moral purity to moral corruption—the destruction of error by the potency of truth—the overthrow of prejudice by the power of love—and the abolition of slavery by the spirit of repentance.

Their grievances, great as they were, were trifling in comparison with the wrongs and sufferings of those for whom we plead. Our fathers were never slaves—never bought and sold like cattle—never shut out from the light of knowledge and religion—never subjected to the lash of brutal taskmasters.

But those, for whose emancipation we are striving—constituting at the present time at least one-sixth part of our countrymen—are recognized by law, and treated by their fellow-beings, as marketable commodities, as goods and chattels, as brute beasts; are plundered daily of the fruits of their toil without redress; really enjoy no constitutional nor legal protection from licentious and murderous outrages upon their persons; and are ruthlessly torn asunder—the tender babe from the arms of its frantic mother—the heart-broken wife from her weeping husband—at the caprice or pleasure of irresponsible tyrants. For the crime of having a dark complexion, they suffer the pangs of hunger, the infliction of stripes, the ignominy of brutal servitude. They are kept in heathenish darkness by laws expressly enacted to make their instruction a criminal offence.

These are the prominent circumstances in the condition of more than two millions of our people, the proof of which may be found in thousands of indisputable facts, and in the laws of the slaveholding States.

Beliefs

Hence we maintain—that, in view of the civil and religious privileges of this nation, the guilt of its oppression is unequalled by any other on the face of the earth; and, therefore, that it is bound to repent instantly, to undo the heavy burdens, and to let the oppressed go free.

We further maintain—that no man has a right to enslave or imbrute his brother—to hold or acknowledge him, for one moment, as a piece of merchandise—to keep back his hire by fraud—or to brutalize his mind, by denying him the means of intellectual, social and moral improvement.

The right to enjoy liberty is inalienable. To invade it is to usurp the prerogative of Jehovah. Every man has a right to his own body—to the products of his own labor—to the protection of law—and to the common advantages of society. It is piracy to buy or steal a native African, and subject him to servitude. Surely, the sin is as great to enslave an American as an African.

Therefore we believe and affirm—that there is no difference, in principle, between the African slave trade and American slavery;

That every American citizen, who detains a human being in involuntary bondage as his property, is, according to Scripture (Ex. xxi, 16), a man-stealer;

That the slaves ought instantly to be set free, and brought under the protection of law;

That if they had lived from the time of Pharaoh down to the present period, and had been entailed through successive generations, their right to be free could never have been alienated, but their claims would have constantly risen in solemnity;

That all those laws which are now in force, admitting the right of slavery, are therefore, before God, utterly null and void; being an audacious usurpation of the Divine prerogative, a daring infringement on the law of nature, a base overthrow of the very foundations of the social compact, a complete extinction of all the relations, endearments and obligations of mankind, and a presumptuous transgression of all the holy commandments; and that therefore they ought instantly to be abrogated.

We further believe and affirm—that all persons of color, who possess the qualifications which are demanded of others, ought to be admitted forthwith to the enjoyment of the same privileges, and the exercise of the same prerogatives, as others; and that the paths of preferment, of wealth, and of intelligence, should be opened as widely to them as to persons of a white complexion.

We maintain that no compensation should be given to the planters emancipating their slaves;

Because it would be a surrender of the great fundamental principle, that man cannot hold property in man;

Because slavery is a crime, and therefore is not an article to be sold;

Because the holders of slaves are not the just proprietors of what they claim; freeing the slave is not depriving them of property, but restoring it to its rightful owner; it is not wronging the master, but righting the slave—restoring him to himself;

Because immediate and general emancipation would only

destroy nominal, rot real property; it would not amputate a limb or break a bone of the slaves, but by infusing motives into their breasts, would make them doubly valuable to the masters as free laborers; and

Because, if compensation is to be given at all, it should be given to the outraged and guiltless slaves, and not to those who have plundered and abused them.

We regard as delusive, cruel and dangerous, any scheme of expatriation which pretends to aid, either directly or indirectly, in the emancipation of the slaves, or to be a substitute for the immediate and total abolition of slavery.

We fully and unanimously recognise the sovereignty of each State, to legislate exclusively on the subject of the slavery which is tolerated within its limits; we concede that Congress, under the present national compact, has no right to interfere with any of the slave States, in relation to this momentous subject:

But we maintain that Congress has a right, and is solemnly bound, to suppress the domestic slave trade between the several States, and to abolish slavery in those portions of our territory which the Constitution has placed under its exclusive jurisdiction.

We also maintain that there are, at the present time, the highest obligations resting upon the people of the free States to remove slavery by moral and political action, as prescribed in the Constitution of the United States. They are now living under a pledge of their tremendous physical force, to fasten the galling fetters of tyranny upon the limbs of millions in the Southern States; they are liable to be called at any moment to suppress a general insurrection of the slaves; they authorize the slave owner to vote for three-fifths of his slaves as property, and thus enable him to perpetuate his oppression; they support a standing army at the South for its protection; and they seize the slave, who has escaped into their territories, and send him back to be tortured by an enraged master or a brutal driver. This relation to slavery is criminal, and full of danger: IT MUST BE BROKEN UP.

These are our views and principles—these our designs and measures. With entire confidence in the overruling justice of

God, we plant ourselves upon the Declaration of our Independence and the truths of Divine Revelation, as upon the Everlasting Rock.

We shall organize Anti-Slavery Societies, if possible, in every city, town and village in our land.

We shall send forth agents to lift up the voice of remonstrance, of warning, of entreaty, and of rebuke.

We shall circulate, unsparingly and extensively, anti-slavery tracts and periodicals.

We shall enlist the pulpit and the press in the cause of the suffering and the dumb.

We shall aim at a purification of the churches from all participation in the guilt of slavery.

We shall encourage the labor of freemen rather than that of slaves, by giving a preference to their productions; and

We shall spare no exertions nor means to bring the whole nation to speedy repentance.

Our trust for victory is solely in God. We may be personally defeated, but our principles never! Truth, Justice, Reason, Humanity, must and will gloriously triumph. Already a host is coming up to the help of the Lord against the mighty, and the prospect before us is full of encouragement.

Submitting this Declaration to the candid examination of the people of this country, and of the friends of liberty throughout the world, we hereby affix our signatures to it; pledging ourselves that, under the guidance and by the help of Almighty God, we will do all that in us lies, consistently with this Declaration of our principles, to overthrow the most execrable system of slavery that has ever been witnessed upon earth; to deliver our land from its deadliest curse; to wipe out the foulest stain which rests upon our national escutcheon; and to secure to the colored population of the United States, all the rights and privileges which belong to them as men, and as Americans—come what may to our persons, our interests, or our reputation—whether we live to witness the triumph of Liberty, Justice and Humanity, or perish untimely as martyrs in this great, benevolent, and holy cause.

Religion and Reform

JOHN R. MCKIVIGAN AND MITCHELL SNAY

John R. McKivigan is professor of history at West Virginia University, and Mitchell Snay is an associate professor of history at Denison University. McKivigan and Snay are the editors of *Religion and the Antebellum Debate over Slavery*. The book's introduction, from which this selection is excerpted, points out that religious conviction was often a motivating factor among antislavery advocates. However, the professors continue, having faith did not always equate to possessing an abolitionist outlook, as many slaveholders felt deeply that Christian ideals did not conflict with possessing slaves. Churches, often caught in the middle of the debate, tried desperately not to alienate any of their congregation. Many churches stipulated that they would not take a stand in what they deemed political or secular matters. Others openly rejected the abolitionists as too condemning of their fellow Christians.

At the time of the rise of the modern abolitionist movement in the early 1830s, northern churches had just completed a significant recovery in strength and prestige. For a few years after the Revolution, the moral authority of the clergy and churches seemed seriously weakened by the social disruption caused by that conflict and by the popularity of the deistic beliefs of many of the Founding Fathers. Around the turn of the century, however, the revivalistic enthusiasm of the Second Great Awakening had restored waning church attendance and support for religion. During the period from 1800 to 1830, Methodist membership increased sevenfold, Baptist membership tripled, and Congregationalist membership doubled. In 1850, approximately one out of every seven or eight Americans was an official member of a denomination, and two or three times that number attended church with some regularity. According to the testimony of both contemporary observers and historians, the revitalized churches exerted significant influences over the individual, social, and even political and economic behavior of millions of Americans....

VIEWS OF SLAVERY IN THE NORTHERN CHURCHES

Despite . . . considerable differences in theology, polity, and demographic makeup, northern churches shared a proslavery heritage. With the exception of only a few pietistic sects, such as the Society of Friends or the Quakers, northern churches in the colonial era had displayed a high degree of toleration toward the institution in both the North and the South. In the aftermath of the Revolution, however, the wide acceptance of Enlightenment concepts regarding natural rights and human liberty led several denominations to incorporate condemnations of slaveholding in their disciplines. But this early burst of antislavery vigor in the churches barely lasted out the century, and few denominations actually enforced disciplinary actions against slave-owning members. What remained of church antislavery sentiment concentrated instead on such ameliorative programs as missionary work among the slaves and advocacy of colonization.

The immediate emancipation movement therefore came into direct conflict with the toleration of slavery by the vast majority of churches. At the root of this confrontation were fundamental disagreements about the morality of slavery and the churches' proper role in the face of this institution. Heavily influenced by contemporary evangelical trends, immediate abolitionists considered slaveholding a sin from which true repentance required instant voluntary renunciation. Because they regarded slave-owning as sinful, the abolitionists argued that the churches must subject the practice to the same disciplinary action as intemperance, adultery, theft, and other immoral practices. Opponents of slavery hoped that the slaveholders' consciences might be reached if threatened with the mortal odium of ejection from the religious community. The abolitionists sought to persuade the churches to take an unqualified stand against slavery. Their opponents held contrary views in varying degrees that formed a kind of continuum.

An unabashedly proslavery faction defended slavery on scriptural grounds, claiming that both revealed and natural religion sanctioned slavery. In denominations in which evangelicalism's impact was weak, there was usually a conservative element that declared slavery a secular matter toward which religious bodies should remain neutral. Almost as conservative were northern church members who had personal objections to slavery but felt that the denominations should defer to southern churchgoers on this issue. Perhaps the largest group of northern churchgoers could be classified as antislavery moderates. This faction acknowledged slavery as an evil institution and believed that the churches should support gradualistic programs, such as colonization, and later, nonextensionism, to end it. These moderates, however, objected to the abolitionists' blanket attacks on the character of slaveholders and to their efforts to expel southerners from the churches. . . .

OBSTACLES FOR ABOLITIONISTS

Even moderate antislavery church leaders dissented from the abolitionist description of slaveholding as an unqualified sin. These antislavery moderates contended that some slave owners could not be held morally accountable for their actions. One expression of this viewpoint acknowledged grounds on which slaveholders could escape the guilt attached to their position. For example, if an individual became an owner of slaves involuntarily, perhaps through inheritance, and found himself legally prohibited from manumitting them, he was not to be adjudged a sinner. Antislavery moderates sometimes claimed that a master who recognized the evil of slavery would be morally correct to delay freeing his slaves if circumstances made such an action detrimental to their welfare.

Another subject of debate was the reformer's demand that the religious institutions cease all practices that lent moral forbearance to slavery. In particular, most denominational leaders rejected abolitionist proposals to bar slaveholders from church membership regardless of the Christian piety they evinced. Liturgical denominations, such as Roman Catholic and Episcopalian, refused to deny fellowship to slaveholders because the idea that individuals could be held responsible for the sins of other church members was contrary to their established doctrines. In many denominations, sweeping guidelines on acceptable moral behavior were opposed as infringements upon the local autonomy of lower judicatories. Even moderate antislavery church members argued that the slaveholders' consciences could be enlightened better inside the religious bodies than outside them.

Other objections to the abolitionists' religious principles and goals related to more worldly considerations. Many church leaders hesitated to endorse any position on slavery that might drive away southern members. Such caution is attributable both to feelings of denominational pride and to fears that divisive public quarrels would jeopardize confidence in the church's moral leadership. Both popular revivalists and local ministers complained that preaching against slavery would interfere with their missionary and other purely religious work.

A final major obstacle faced by abolitionists in the churches was the strong support given by their moderate rivals to more gradualistic antislavery programs. When abolitionism and proslaveryism began making their disruptive appeals, antislavery moderates deprecated both views as "ultraism" and professed to maintain the scripturally grounded, traditional position of the churches toward slavery. Antislavery moderates placed greater confidence than did abolitionists in the reasonableness and Christian character of the slaveholder. Church leaders opposed to abolitionism rejected calls for immediate emancipation and favored more gradual programs, including compensation for masters, colonization, and apprenticeship periods to prepare slaves for the responsibilities of freedom.

FACTORS IN THE ANTISLAVERY DEBATE

Analysis of the northern churches' response to this debate over slavery reveals that a number of sociocultural and institutional factors interacted with theological issues to erect complex barriers against the success of abolitionist efforts. To a large extent, the acceptance of abolitionism by a particular religious body seems to be correlated with its position on certain broader theological issues. The degree to which evangelical doctrines affected a denomination generally determined its receptivity to abolitionist arguments. For example, the liturgical churches, such as those of Catholics and those of Episcopalians, and liberal churches, such as the Unitarians, all objected to one or more aspects of abolitionists' evangelically inspired claim that slaveholders were inherently sinners and that the churches had a moral obligation to purify their communions by expelling them. But even a strong evangelical orientation was no guarantee of denominational adoption of abolitionist principles. The evangelical doctrine of human perfectionism popular in some denominations encouraged involvement in benevolent and reform movements, but in other denominations, including Methodism, it caused a more inward-directed striving for holiness.

Theological attitudes governing the composition of church membership also seemed to correlate with a predisposition to move toward or away from abolitionism. The liturgical denominations with considerable tolerance for human imperfection generally rejected the abolitionist condemnation of the slaveholder as sinner. At the other extreme, religious bodies with a desire for a scrupulously purified communion of believers generally rejected abolitionist principles that would add new, nontheological tests of fitness from membership. Abolitionists fared best among denominations that struck a balance between a near-universal and a highly exclusive membership standard.

A denomination's tradition with regard to social activism had a discernable impact on its response to abolitionism. Episcopalians, New England Congregationalists, and Unitarians, with their status as established churches, were slow to shed their defensive attitude toward the existing social order. These denominations were cautious about taking any position on controversial issues that might jeopardize their links to the social and economic elites. Another category of churches disinclined toward social activism were small sects with pietistic traditions, such as the Quakers. These sects not only preferred to withdraw from worldly corruption but also discouraged their members from associating with nonmembers in any projects with religious overtones.

Ecclesiastical structure also played an important role in the progress abolitionists made in different denominations. The decentralized structure of denominations, such as the Baptists, Congregationalists, and Unitarians, delegated to local jurisdictions the authority to determine standards for membership. As a result, abolitionists were able to attract numerous converts in those churches but remained powerless to establish uniform antislavery practices in them. At the other extreme, Episcopalian, Roman Catholic, and other denominations where the clergy possessed all or nearly all authority, provided abolitionists no direct means to influence church practices. It was in denominations with a federated structure (e.g., the Presbyterians and Methodists) that the abolitionists were able to make greatest headway because once in control of a few local judicatories they could dispatch delegates and address petitions to higher authorities to demand the establishment of strict antislavery rules.

Another aspect of church government that affected the abolitionists' campaign was the power of a denominational hierarchy to suppress antislavery debate within church councils. Roman Catholic and Episcopalian bishops forbade their clergy to participate in organized abolitionist activities. Methodist bishops lacked the same sweeping authority but persuaded local conferences to discipline or expel persistent antislavery agitators from the ranks of their preachers and lay moderators. Through its control over all editorial appointments, the Methodist General Conference also was able to keep abolitionist articles out of its large network of newspapers and periodicals. Even in denominations with substantial local inde-

pendence, conservatives found means to discourage abolitionist agitation. In New England, Congregational ministerial associations tried but failed to bar itinerant abolitionist speakers
from their pulpits. Among Baptists, abolitionist influence was
curtailed by a systematic purging of antislavery agitators from
all positions of influence in the denominational missionary and
in publication societies.

SOUTHERN INFLUENCES, ABOLITIONIST FRICTION

Southern influence likewise proved a conservative force in
many churches. In denominational and interdenominational
benevolent organizations, such as missionary or Bible societies,
there was a reluctance even to consider abolitionist arguments
because southerners were major financial patrons of those organizations. In addition, many northern clergymen had been
educated with slave owners in colleges and seminaries and had
taught or preached in the slave states at some point in their ca-
reers, and, as a result, they were disinclined to agree with blanket condemnations of their intimate acquaintances.

The dedication of many northern church leaders to the existing political status quo caused them to resist abolitionism in
religious councils. Bishop Beverly Waugh warned New England Methodists that the abolitionist agitation risked "the destruction of our beautiful and excellent form of civil and political government, after it has cost the labor, treasure, and blood
of our fathers to establish it." Antiabolitionist northern Baptists rejected condemnations of slaveholding because such a
course could enflame political as well as religious sectionalism;
they argued that "as patriots, we must cherish religious union,
as one of the strongest . . . of the bonds that hold together the
Union of these States."

Finally, southern influence was felt through the great economic power that slavery exerted over the entire nation. Many
northern merchants, bankers, and cotton-mill investors had
large financial interests in slavery. As major contributors to religious and benevolent institutions, these men used their in-

fluence to promote the status quo where slavery was concerned and thus to operate against antislavery programs that would reflect negatively on the character of their enterprises. The power of these prosouthern forces proved to be a major obstacle to antislavery advances in churches in urban, commercial, and manufacturing centers across the entire North.

The strength and determination of the antiabolitionist opposition in the northern churches produced great friction in the abolitionist ranks and contributed to that movement's schism over tactics in 1840. While followers of William Lloyd Garrison denounced the churches as hopelessly corrupted by slavery and turned to more exclusively secular tactics, many other abolitionists continued the campaign to reform northern religious institutions. This second abolitionist faction worked with well-organized denominational antislavery movements. Methodist, Baptist, and Presbyterian abolitionists lobbied their denominations to expel slaveholders. These movements had an important impact in fomenting the sectional schisms of the Methodist and Baptist churches in the mid-1840s and the New School Presbyterians in 1857. Even following those divisions, however, abolitionists complained that the northern church branches still tolerated slavery. As evidence, abolitionists noted that none of these denominations condemned slaveholding as sinful and that each retained thousands of border state slave owners in their fellowship. . . .

POLITICAL INFLUENCES

Political antislavery activities beginning in the 1840s also had important influence on the abolitionist campaign in the churches. The men who founded the first abolitionist political vehicle, the Liberty Party, believed antislavery efforts in the political and religious spheres to be linked inseparably. The earliest antislavery politicians condemned slave-owning as a sin and endorsed nonfellowship with slaveholders. Even the moderate antislavery arguments of the later Free Soil and Republican Parties for nonextension encouraged northerners to view slavery as a morally unacceptable institution. As a result of their close connection, the political and ecclesiastical antislavery movements reinforced each other's growth in the 1840s and 1850s.

Although most northern denominations still stopped short of adopting abolitionist principles and practices, there was evidence that abolitionist pressure increased antislavery sentiment in the northern churches during the 1840s and 1850s. Only the traditionally antislavery denominations (including the Quakers and Freewill Baptists and a few new "comeouter" sects founded by abolitionists) condemned all slaveholders as sinners and refused to share religious fellowship with them before the beginning of the Civil War. The secession of southern members from the New School Presbyterian and Methodist Episcopal churches in the immediate prewar years effectively ended the fellowship of slaveholders, but these major churches still refrained from making any formal endorsement of abolitionism. Although many Unitarians, Baptists, and Congregationalists strengthened their testimony against the evils of slavery, none of these denominations came up to abolitionist standards by severing all ties with slaveholders. The liturgical denominations remained firm in their long-standing position that slavery was a morally neutral and exclusively secular question. Despite considerable antislavery progress in many denominations, abolitionism remained a minority viewpoint in the northern church in 1860.

The coming of the Civil War broke down much of the northern churches' resistance to taking aggressive antislavery actions. The secession of the southern states led many denominations to acknowledge the moral corruption inherent in a slaveholding society. Wartime antisouthern sentiment even led the Methodist Episcopal Church to adopt a discipline barring slave owners from membership. After initial hesitation, most denominations responded to abolitionist entreaties to endorse emancipation. With the exception of liturgical denominations, northern churches lobbied the president and Congress during the war to put an end to slavery. Before the war's end, many northern church leaders also enlisted in abolitionist efforts to reinforce emancipation with freedmen's aid and anti–racial discrimination programs.

Antislavery Tactics

HOWARD ZINN

Professor emeritus of political science Howard Zinn, of Boston University, is both a scholar and a social activist. The following selection is from an essay in a 1965 work, edited by Martin Duberman, entitled *The Antislavery Vanguard: New Essays on the Abolitionists.* In this piece, Zinn reveals a sympathetic view of the abolitionists and the tactics they used to promote their cause. He maintains that the nature of fighting an extremely vile institution like slavery called for radical action. This was because, as the abolitionists themselves realized, the average American untouched by slavery firsthand needed to be shocked out of complacency and driven to take a stand on the issue.

There is no denying the anger, the bitterness, the irascibility of the abolitionists. William Lloyd Garrison, dean of them all, wrote in blood in the columns of the *Liberator* and breathed fire from speakers' platforms all over New England. He shocked people: "I am ashamed of my country." He spoke abroad in brutal criticism of America: "I accuse the land of my nativity of insulting the majesty of Heaven with the greatest mockery that was ever exhibited to man." He burned the Constitution before several thousand witnesses on the lawn at Framingham, calling it "source and parent of all other atrocities—a covenant with death and an agreement with hell" and spurred the crowd to echo "Amen!"

He provoked his opponents outrageously, and the South became apoplectic at the mention of his name. South Carolina offered $1,500 for conviction of any white person circulating the *Liberator,* and the Georgia legislature offered $500 for the arrest and conviction of Garrison. Garrison's wife feared constantly that reward-seekers would lie in wait for her husband on his way back from a meeting and snatch him off to Georgia.

EXTREMIST ABOLITIONISTS

Wendell Phillips, richer, and from a distinguished Boston family, was no softer. "Don't shilly-shally, Wendell," his wife whispered to him as he mounted the speakers' platform, and he never did. The anger that rose in him one day in 1835 as he watched Boston bluebloods drag Garrison through the streets never left him, and it remained focused on what he considered America's unbearable evil—slavery. "The South is one great brothel," he proclaimed.

Gradualism was not for Phillips. "No sir, we may not trifle or dally. . . . Revolution is the only thing, the only power, that ever worked out freedom for any people." The piety of New England did not intimidate him: "The American church— what is it? A synagogue of Satan." He scorned patriotic pride: "They sell a little image of us in the markets of Mexico, with a bowie knife in one side of the girdle, and a Colt's revolver in the other, a huge loaf of bread in the left hand, and a slave whip in the right. That is America!"

Phillips did not use the language of nonresistance as did Garrison. On that same green where Garrison burned the Constitution, Phillips said: "We are very small in numbers; we have got no wealth; we have got no public opinion behind us; the only thing that we can do is, like the eagle, simply to fly at our enemy, and pick out his eyes." And: "I want no man for President of these States . . . who has not got his hand half clenched, and means to close it on the jugular vein of the slave system the moment he reaches it, and has a double-edged dagger in the other hand, in case there is any missing in the strangulation."

But even Garrison and Phillips seem moderate against the figure of John Brown, lean and lusty, with two wives and twenty children, filled with enough anger for a regiment of agitators, declaring personal war on the institution of slavery. Speeches and articles were for others. The old man studied military strategy, pored over maps of the Southern terrain, raised money for arms, and planned the forcible liberation of slaves through rebellion and guerrilla warfare. On Pottowattomie Creek in the bleeding Kansas of 1856, on the Sabbath, he had struck one night at an encampment of proslavery men, killing five with a cold ferocity. On his way to the gallows, after the raid on the Harpers Ferry arsenal in Virginia in the fall of 1859, he wrote: "I John Brown am now quite certain that the crimes of this guilty land will never be purged away; but with Blood."

The Negro abolitionist, Frederick Douglass, newly freed from slavery himself, and long a believer in "moral suasion" to free others, talked with John Brown at his home in 1847 and came away impressed by his arguments. Two years later, Douglass told a Boston audience: "I should welcome the intelligence tomorrow, should it come, that the slaves had risen in the South, and that the sable arms which had been engaged in beautifying and adorning the South, were engaged in spreading death and devastation." He thought the Harpers Ferry plan wild, and would not go along; yet, to the end, he maintained that John Brown at Harpers Ferry began the war that ended slavery. "Until this blow was struck, the prospect for freedom was dim, shadowy, and uncertain. . . . When John Brown stretched forth his arm the sky was cleared."

These are the extremists. Did they hurt or help the cause of freedom? Or did they, if helping this cause, destroy some other value, like human life, lost in huge numbers in the Civil War? To put it another way, were they a hindrance rather than a help in abolishing Slavery? Did their activities bring a solution at too great a cost? . . .

NATURE OF THE CAUSE

If the notion of "extremism" is too nebulous to sustain a firm judgment on a goal or a tactic, how do we judge? One point of reference might be the nature and severity of the problem. . . . While more modest evils might be dislodged by a few sharp words, the elimination of slavery clearly required more drastic action. The abolitionists did not deceive themselves that they were gentle and temperate; they quite consciously measured their words to the enormity of the evil.

Garrison said in 1833: "How, then, ought I to feel and speak and write, in view of a system which is red with innocent blood drawn from the bodies of millions of my countrymen by the scourge of brutal drivers. . . . My soul should be, as it is, on fire. I should thunder, I should lighten, I should blow the trumpet of alarm long and loud. I should use just such language as is most descriptive of the crime."

How evil was slavery? It was a complex phenomenon, different in every individual instance, with the treatment of slaves varying widely. But the whole range of variation was in a general framework of unspeakable inhumanity. Even at its "best," slavery was a ferocious attack on man's dignity. It was described matter-of-factly by a supporter of the system, Judge Edmund Ruffin of North Carolina: "Such services can only be expected from one who has no will of his own; who surrenders his will in implicit obedience to another. Such obedience is the consequence only of uncontrolled authority over the body. There is no remedy. This discipline belongs to the state of slavery. . . . It constitutes the curse of slavery to both the bond and the free portion of our population. But it is inherent in the relation of master and slave."

And at its worst, slavery was, as Allan Nevins has said: ". . . the greatest misery, the greatest wrong, the greatest curse to white and black alike that America has ever known." Ads for fugitive slaves in the Southern press (5,400 advertisements a year) contained descriptions like the following to aid apprehension: ". . . Stamped N.E. on the breast and having both small toes cut off. . . . Has some scars on his back that show above the skin, caused by the whip. . . . Has an iron band around his neck. . . . Has a ring of iron on his left foot. . . . Has on a large neck iron, with a huge pair of horns and a large bar or band of iron on his left leg. . . . Branded on the left cheek, thus 'R', and a piece is taken off her left ear on the same side; the same letter is branded on the inside of both legs." One plantation diary read: ". . . whipped every field hand this evening." A Natchez slave who attacked a white man was chained to a tree and burned alive.

Against this, how mild Garrison's words seem. . . .

THE PLACE OF COMPROMISE

The argument over the wisdom of radical agitation in the tactics of social reform was aptly expressed in Boston in pre–Civil War years by two leading figures. Samuel May, speaking of Garrison, said: ". . . he will shake our nation to its center, but he will shake slavery out of it." Reverend Lyman Beecher said: "True wisdom consists in advocating a cause only so far as the community will sustain the reformer." The agitator, declare the moderate reformers, shakes so hard that he makes compromise impossible, alienates friends, and delays rather than speeds the coming of reform.

Compromise was not disdained by the abolitionists; they were fully conscious of the fact that the outcome of any social struggle is almost always some form of compromise. But they were also aware of that which every intelligent radical knows: that to compromise in advance is to vitiate at the outset that power for progress which only the radical propels into the debate. [James Russell] Lowell put this most vividly, declaring that the abolitionists "are looked upon as peculiarly ungrateful and impracticable if they do not devote their entire energies to soliciting nothing, and express a thankfulness amounting almost to rapture when they get it."

The abolitionist took an advanced position so that even if pushed back by compromise, substantial progress would result. Garrison wrote: "Urge immediate abolition as earnestly as we may, it will be gradual abolition in the end." And Phillips said: "If we would get half a loaf, we must demand the whole of it." The Emancipation Proclamation itself was a compromise, the tortured product of a long battle between radicals and moderates in and out of the Lincoln administration, and only the compelling force of the abolitionist intransigeants made it come as soon as it did.

Two factors demand recognition by moderates who disdain

"extreme" positions on the ground that compromise is necessary. One is the above-mentioned point that the early projection of an advanced position ensures a compromise on more favorable terms than would be the case where the timorous reformer compromises at the start (in which case the result is a compromise upon a compromise, since he will be forced to retreat even from his retreat after all the forces are calculated at the social weighing-in). The other is that there is a huge difference between the passive wisher-for-change who quietly adds up the vectors and makes a decision as to which is the composite of all existing forces, and the active reformer who pushes so hard *in the course of adding-up* that the composite itself is changed. The latter—the radical—is viewing compromise as a dynamic process, in which his own actions are part of the total force being calculated. He bases his estimate of what is possible on a graph in which his own action and its consequences are calculated from the first.

MODERATE VS. RADICAL TACTICS

Does the agitator alienate potential allies by the extremism of his demands, or the harshness of his language? Lewis Tappan, the wealthy New Yorker who financed many abolitionist activities, wrote anxiously to George Thompson, the British abolitionist: "The fact need not be concealed from you that several emancipationists so disapprove of the harsh, and, as they think, the unchristian language of *The Liberator,* that they do not feel justified in upholding it." This, in general, was the feeling of the Executive Committee of the American Anti-Slavery Society in the early years of the movement. . . .

When friends of the reformers rail against harsh words or strong action (as the American Anti-Slavery Society did against Garrison) it is clear that they themselves will not be put off from reform because of it, but fear the effects on others. And if neither extreme opposition nor hard-and-fast friends can be moved by tactics of moderation, this leaves, as a decisive group, that large part of the population which is at neither end of the ideological spectrum, which moves back and forth across the center line, depending on circumstances.

Garrison was quite aware that most of the American population to which he was appealing was not sympathetic with his views, and he was completely conscious of how distant were his own fiery convictions from those of the average American. But he was persuaded, as were Phillips and other leading abolitionists (John Brown felt it, and acted it, if he did not express it intellectually) that only powerful surges of words and feelings could move white people from their complacency about the slave question. He said once in Philadelphia: "Sir, slavery will not be overthrown without excitement, a most tremendous excitement." He must lash with words, he felt, those Americans who had never felt the whip of a slaveowner. To his friend Samuel May, who urged him to keep more cool, saying: "Why, you are all on fire," Garrison replied: "Brother May, I have need to be all on fire, for I have mountains of ice about me to melt."

We have the historical record as a check on whether the vituperative language of Garrison, the intemperate appeals of Wendell Phillips, hurt or advanced the popular sentiment against slavery. In the 1830's a handful of men cried out against slavery and were beaten, stoned, and shot to death by their Northern compatriots. By 1849, antislavery sentiment was clearly increasing, and some of the greatest minds and voices in America were speaking out for abolition. Lowell asked curtly of those who charged the abolitionists with retarding the movement: ". . . has there really been a change of public opinion for the worse, either at the North or the South, since the *Liberator* came into existence eighteen years ago?" And by 1860, with millions of Americans convinced that slavery was an evil, open insurrection by John Brown brought more public support than had the mere words of Garrison thirty years before.

Martyrs and Mob Violence

WENDELL PHILLIPS

Wendell Phillips (1811–1884) was a leading abolitionist, a lawyer, and a great orator. Phillips delivered this speech on December 8, 1837, before a crowd at Faneuil Hall in Boston. A meeting was called there to protest the murder of abolitionist editor Elijah P. Lovejoy in a (proslavery) mob riot in Alton, Illinois. Phillips rose to speak after the Attorney General of the Commonwealth delivered a diatribe against abolitionists that portrayed Lovejoy as a fool who died in vain. In his well-received address, Phillips responds to the proslavery advocates while posing powerful rhetorical questions about individual rights and the freedom of the press. He draws comparisons between the spirit of abolitionism and the spirit of the American Revolution.

M r. Chairman—We have met for the freest discussion of these resolutions, and the events which gave rise to them. [Cries of "Question," "Hear him," "Go on," "No gagging," etc.] I hope I shall be permitted to express my surprise at the sentiments of the last speaker—surprise not only at such sentiments from such a man, but at the applause they have received within these walls. A comparison has been drawn between the events of the Revolution and the tragedy at Alton. We have heard it asserted here, in Faneuil Hall, that Great Britain had a right to tax the Colonies, and we have heard the mob at Alton, the drunken murderers of Lovejoy, compared to those patriot fathers who threw the tea overboard! [Great applause.] Fellow-citizens, is this Faneuil Hall doctrine? ["No, no!"] The mob at Alton were met to wrest from a citizen his just rights—met to resist the laws. We have been told that our fathers did the same; and the glorious mantle of Revolutionary precedent has been thrown over the mobs of our day. To make out their title to such defence, the gentleman says that the British Parliament had a right to tax these Colonies. It is manifest that, without this, his parallel falls to the ground; for Lovejoy had stationed himself within constitutional bulwarks. He was not only defending the freedom of the press, but he was under his own roof, in arms with the sanction of the civil authority. The men who assailed him went against and over the laws. The mob, as the gentleman terms it—mob, forsooth! Certainly we sons of the tea-spillers are a marvellously patient generation—the "orderly mob" which assembled in the Old South to destroy the tea were met to resist, not the laws, but illegal exactions. Shame on the American who calls the tea-tax and stamp-act laws! Our fathers resisted, not the King's prerogative, but the King's usurpation. To find any other account, you must read our Revolutionary history upside down. Our State archives are loaded with arguments of John Adams to prove the taxes laid by the British Parliament unconstitutional—beyond its power. It was not till this was made out that the men of New England rushed to arms. The arguments of the Council Chamber and the House of Representatives preceded and sanctioned the contest. To draw the conduct of our ancestors into a precedent for mobs, for a right to resist laws we ourselves have enacted, is an insult to their memory. The difference between the excitements of those days and our own, which the gentleman in kindness to the latter has overlooked, is simply this: the men of that day went for the right, as secured by the laws. They were the people rising to sustain the laws and constitution of the Province. The rioters of our day go for their own wills, right or wrong. Sir, when I heard the gentleman lay down principles which place the murderers of Alton side by side with Otis and Hancock, with Quincy and Adams, I thought those pictured lips [pointing to the portraits in the Hall] would have broken into voice to rebuke the recreant American—the slanderer of the dead. [Great applause and counterapplause.] The gentleman said that he should sink into insignificance if he dared to gainsay the principles of these resolutions. Sir, for the sentiments he has uttered, on soil consecrated by the prayers of Puritans and the blood of patriots, the earth should have yawned and swallowed him up. . . .

DENOUNCING THE ALTON MOB

Another ground has been taken to excuse the mob, and throw doubt and discredit on the conduct of Lovejoy and his associates. Allusion has been made to what lawyers understand very well—the "conflict of laws." We are told that nothing but the Mississippi River rolls between St. Louis and Alton; and the conflict of laws somehow or other gives the citizens of the former a right to find fault with the defender of the press for publishing his opinions so near their limits. Will the gentleman venture that argument before lawyers? How the laws of the two States could be said to come into conflict in such circumstances I question whether any lawyer in this audience can explain or understand. No matter whether the line that divides one sovereign State from another be an imaginary one or ocean-wide, the moment you cross it the State you leave is blotted out of existence, so far as you are concerned. The Czar might as well claim to control the deliberations of Faneuil Hall, as the laws of Missouri demand reverence, or the shadow of obedience, from an inhabitant of Illinois.

I must find some fault with the statement which has been made of the events at Alton. It has been asked why Lovejoy and his friends did not appeal to the executive—trust their defence to the police of the city. It has been hinted that, from hasty and ill-judged excitement, the men within the building provoked a quarrel, and that he fell in the course of it, one mob resisting another. Recollect, Sir, that they did act with the approbation and sanction of the Mayor. In strict truth, there was no executive to appeal to for protection. The Mayor acknowledged that he could not protect them. They asked him if it was lawful for them to defend themselves. He told them it was, and sanctioned their assembling in arms to do so. They were not, then, a mob; they were not merely citizens defending their own property; they were in some sense the *posse comitatus,* adapted for the occasion into the police of the city, acting under the order of the magistrate. It was civil authority resisting lawless violence. Where, then, was the imprudence? Is the doctrine to be sustained here, that it is *imprudent* for men to aid magistrates in executing the laws?

Men are continually asking each other, Had Lovejoy a right to resist? Sir, I protest against the question, instead of answering it. Lovejoy did not resist, in the sense they mean. He did not throw himself back on the natural right of self-defence. He did not cry anarchy and let slip the dogs of civil war, careless of the horrors which would follow.

Sir, as I understand this affair, it was not an individual protecting his property; it was not one body of armed men resisting another, and making the streets of a peaceful city run blood with their contentions. It did not bring back the scenes in some old Italian cities, where family met family, and faction met faction, and mutually trampled the laws under foot. No; the men in that house were regularly *enrolled,* under the sanction of the Mayor. There being no militia in Alton, about seventy men were enrolled with the approbation of the Mayor. These relieved each other every other night. About thirty men were in arms on the night of the sixth, when the press was landed. The next evening, it was not thought necessary to summon more than half that number; among these was Lovejoy. It was, therefore, you perceive, Sir, the police of the city resisting rioters—civil government breasting itself to the shock of lawless men.

Here is no question about the right of self-defence. It is in fact simply this: Has the civil magistrate a right to put down a riot?

Some persons seem to imagine that anarchy existed at Alton from the commencement of these disputes. Not at all. "No one of us," says an eyewitness and a comrade of Lovejoy, "has taken up arms during these disturbances but at the command of the Mayor." Anarchy did not settle down on that devoted city till Lovejoy breathed his last. Till then the law, represented in his person, sustained itself against its foes. When he fell, civil authority was trampled under foot. He had "planted himself on his constitutional rights—appealed to the laws—claimed the protection of the civil authority—taken refuge under the broad shield of the Constitution. When through that he was pierced and fell, he fell but one sufferer in a common catastrophe." He took refuge under the banner of liberty—amid its folds; and when he fell, its glorious stars and stripes, the emblem of free institutions, around which cluster so many heart-stirring memories, were blotted out in the martyr's blood.

THE RIOT

It has been stated, perhaps inadvertently, that Lovejoy or his comrades fired first. This is denied by those who have the best means of knowing. Guns were first fired by the mob. After being twice fired on, those within the building consulted together and deliberately returned the fire. But suppose they did fire first. They had a right so to do; not only the right which every citizen has to defend himself; but the further right which every civil officer has to resist violence. Even if Lovejoy fired the first gun, it would not lessen his claim to our sympathy, or destroy his title to be considered a martyr in defence of a free press. The question now is, Did he act within the Constitution and the laws? The men who fell in State Street on the 5th of March, 1770, did more than Lovejoy is charged with. They were the first assailants. Upon some slight quarrel they pelted the troops with every missile within reach. Did this bate one jot of the eulogy with which Hancock and Warren hallowed their memory, hailing them as the first martyrs in the cause of American liberty?

If, Sir, I had adopted what are called Peace principles, I might lament the circumstances of this case. But all you who believe, as I do, in the right and duty of magistrates to execute the laws, join with me and brand as base hypocrisy the conduct of those who assemble year after year on the 4th of July, to fight over the battles of the Revolution, and yet "Damn with faint praise," or load with obloquy, the memory of this man, who shed his blood in defence of life, liberty, property, and the freedom of the press!

Throughout that terrible night I find nothing to regret but this, that within the limits of our country, civil authority should have been so prostrated as to oblige a citizen to arm in his own defence, and to arm in vain. The gentleman [the Attorney General] says Lovejoy was presumptuous and imprudent—he "died as the fool dieth." And a reverend clergyman of the city tells us that no citizen has a right to publish opinions disagreeable to the community. If any mob follows such publication, on *him* rests its guilt! He must wait, forsooth, till the people come up to it and agree with him! This libel on liberty goes on to say that the want of right to speak as we think is an evil inseparable from republican institutions! If this be so, what are they worth? Welcome the despotism of the Sultan, where one knows what he may publish and what he may not, rather than the tyranny of this many-headed monster, the mob, where we know not what we may do or say, till some fellow-citizen has tried it, and paid for the lesson with his life. This clerical absurdity chooses as a check for the abuses of the press, not the *law,* but the dread of a mob. By so doing, it deprives not only the individual and the minority of their rights, but the majority also, since the expression of *their* opinion may sometimes provoke disturbance from the minority. A few men may make a mob as well as many. The majority, then, have no right, as Christian men, to utter their sentiments, if by any possibility it may lead to a mob! . . .

FREEDOM OF PRESS DEFENDED

Imprudent to defend the liberty of the press! Why? Because the defence was unsuccessful? Does success gild crime into patriotism, and the want of it change heroic self-devotion to imprudence? Was Hampden imprudent when he drew the sword and threw away the scabbard? Yet he, judged by that single hour, was unsuccessful. After a short exile, the race he hated sat again upon the throne.

Imagine yourself present when the first news of Bunker Hill battle reached a New England town. The tale would have run thus: "The patriots are routed—the redcoats victorious—Warren lies dead upon the field." With what scorn would that *Tory* have been received, who should have charged Warren with *imprudence!* Who should have said that, bred a physician, he was "out of place" in that battle, and "died as the *fool dieth*"! [Great applause.] How would the intimation have been received, that Warren and his associates should have waited a better time? But if success be indeed the only criterion of prudence, *Respice finem*—wait till the end.

Presumptuous to assert the freedom of the press on American ground! Is the assertion of such freedom before the age? So much before the age as to leave one no right to make it because it displeases the community? Who invents this libel on his country? It is this very thing which entitles Lovejoy to greater praise. The disputed right which provoked the Revolution—taxation without representation—is far beneath that for which he died. [Here there was a strong and general expression of disapprobation.] One word, gentlemen. As much as *thought* is better than money, so much is the cause in which Lovejoy died nobler than a mere question of taxes. James Otis thundered in this Hall when the King did but touch his *pocket.* Imagine, if you can, his indignant eloquence, had England offered to put a gag upon his lips. [Great applause.]

The question that stirred the Revolution touched our civil interests. *This* concerns us not only as citizens, but as immortal beings. Wrapped up in its fate, saved or lost with it, are not only the voice of the statesman, but the instructions of the pulpit, and the progress of our faith.

The clergy "marvellously out of place" where free speech is battled for—liberty of speech on national sins? Does the gentleman remember that freedom to preach was first gained, dragging in its train freedom to print? I thank the clergy here present, as I reverence their predecessors, who did not so far forget their country in their immediate profession as to deem it duty to separate themselves from the struggle of '76—the

Mayhews and Coopers, who remembered they were citizens before they were clergymen.

Mr. Chairman, from the bottom of my heart I thank that brave little band at Alton for resisting. We must remember that Lovejoy had fled from city to city—suffered the destruction of three presses patiently. At length he took counsel with friends, men of character, of tried integrity, of wide views, of Christian principle. They thought the crisis had come: it was full time to assert the laws. They saw around them, not a community like our own, of fixed habits, of character moulded and settled, but one "in the gristle, not yet hardened into the bone of manhood." The people there, children of our older States, seem to have forgotten the blood-tried principles of their fathers the moment they lost sight of our New England hills. Something was to be done to show them the priceless value of the freedom of the press, to bring back and set right their wandering and confused ideas. He and his advisers looked out on a community, staggering like a drunken man, indifferent to their rights and confused in their feelings. Deaf to argument, haply they might be stunned into sobriety. They saw that of which we cannot judge, the *necessity* of resistance. Insulted law called for it. Public opinion, fast hastening on the downward course, must be arrested.

Does not the event show they judged rightly? Absorbed in a thousand trifles, how has the nation all at once come to a stand? Men begin, as in 1776 and 1640, to discuss principles, to weigh characters, to find out where they are. Haply we may awake before we are borne over the precipice.

I am glad, Sir, to see this crowded house. It is good for us to be here. When Liberty is in danger, Faneuil Hall has the right, it is her duty, to strike the key-note for these United States. I am glad, for one reason, that remarks such as those to which I have alluded have been uttered here. The passage of these resolutions, in spite of this opposition, led by the Attorney-General of the Commonwealth, will show more clearly, more decisively, the deep indignation with which Boston regards this outrage.

Slave Labor vs. Free Labor

LYDIA MARIA CHILD

Lydia Maria Child (1802–1880) was an abolitionist and friend of newspaperman William Lloyd Garrison. She was an accomplished writer and editor. In 1833, just before the founding of the American Anti-Slavery Society, she published *An Appeal in Favor of That Class of Americans Called Africans.* In the book, Child defines her abolitionist stance by refuting proslavery arguments in nearly all aspects of society that slavery has impacted. The selection that follows is from the chapter "Free Labor and Slave Labor—Possibility of Safe Emancipation." In it, Child looks at the economic aspect of slavery and weighs the benefits of free labor against those of slave labor. By showing how slaves lack motivation and have no investment in their work, Child logically concludes how hiring slaves as free men would benefit workers, plantation owners, and the nation's economy in general.

P olitical economists found their systems on those broad and general principles, the application of which has been proved by reason and experience to produce the greatest possible happiness to the greatest number of people. All writers of this class, I believe without exception, prefer free labor to slave labor.

Indeed a very brief glance will show that slavery is inconsistent with *economy,* whether domestic, or political.

COMPARING FREE AND SLAVE LABOR

The slave is bought, sometimes at a very high price; in free labor there is no such investment of capital.—When the slave is ill, a physician must be paid by the owner; the free laborer defrays his own expenses. The children of the slave must be sup-

Excerpted from "Free Labor and Slave Labor," by Lydia Maria Child, *An Appeal in Favor of That Class of Americans Called Africans,* edited by Carolyn L. Karcher (Amherst: University of Massachusetts Press, 1996). Copyright © 1996 by The University of Massachusetts Press. Reprinted with permission.

ported by his master; the free man maintains his own. The slave is to be taken care of in his old age, which his previous habits render peculiarly helpless; the free laborer is hired when he is wanted, and then returns to his home. The slave does not care how slowly or carelessly he works; it is the free man's interest to do his business well and quickly. The slave is indifferent how many tools he spoils; the free man has a motive to be careful. The slave's clothing is indeed very cheap, but it is of no consequence to him how fast it is destroyed—his master *must* keep him covered, and that is all he is likely to do; the hired laborer pays more for his garments, but makes them last three times as long. The free man will be honest for reputation's sake; but reputation will make the slave none the richer, nor invest him with any of the privileges of a human being—while his poverty and sense of wrong both urge him to steal from his master. A salary must be paid to an overseer to compel the slave to work; the free man is impelled by the desire of increasing the comforts of himself and family. Two hired laborers will perform as much work as three slaves; by some it is supposed to be a more correct estimate that slaves perform only *half* as much labor as the same number of free laborers. Finally, *where* slaves are employed, manual industry is a degradation to white people, and indolence becomes the prevailing characteristic.

Slave owners have indeed frequently shown great adroitness in defending this bad system; but, with few exceptions, they base their arguments upon the necessity of continuing slavery because it is already begun. Many of them have openly acknowledged that it was highly injurious to the prosperity of the State.

Henry Clay on Slavery

The Hon. Henry Clay, in his address before the Colonization Society of Kentucky, has given a view of the causes affecting, and likely to affect, slavery in this country, which is very remarkable, for its completeness, its distinctness, and its brevity. The following sentences are quoted from this address: "As a mere laborer, the slave feels that he toils for his master, and not for himself; that the laws do not recognise his capacity to acquire and hold property, which depends altogether upon the pleasure of his proprietor, and that all the fruits of his exertions are reaped by others. He knows that, whether sick or well, in times of scarcity or abundance, his master is bound to provide for him by the all-powerful influence of self-interest. He is generally, therefore, indifferent to the adverse or prosperous fortunes of his master, being contented if he can escape his displeasure or chastisement, by a careless and slovenly performance of his duties.

"This is the state of the relation between master and slave, prescribed by the law of its nature, and founded in the reason

Lydia Maria Child

of things. There are undoubtedly many exceptions, in which the slave dedicates himself to his master with a zealous and generous devotion, and the master to the slave with a parental and affectionate attachment. But it is my purpose to speak of the *general* state of this unfortunate relation.

"That labor is best, in which the laborer knows that he will derive the profits of his industry, that his employment depends upon his diligence, and his reward upon this assiduity. He then has every motive to excite him to exertion, and to animate him in perseverance. He knows that if he is treated badly he can exchange his employer, for one who will better estimate his service; and that whatever he earns is *his,* to be distributed by himself as he pleases, among his wife, and children, and friends, or enjoyed by himself. In a word, he feels that he is a free agent, with rights, and privileges, and sensibilities.

"Wherever the option exists to employ, at an equal hire, free or slave labor, the former will be decidedly preferred, for the reasons already assigned. It is more capable, more diligent, more faithful, and in every respect more worthy of confidence.

"It is believed that nowhere in the *farming* portion of the United States would slave labor be generally employed, if the proprietor were not tempted to raise slaves by the high price of the Southern market, which keeps it up in his own." . . .

I cannot forbear paying a tribute of respect to the venerable Moses Brown, of Providence, Rhode Island, now living in virtuous and vigorous old age. He was a slave owner in early life, and, unless I have been misinformed, a slave dealer, likewise. When his attention became roused to religious subjects, these facts troubled his conscience. He easily and promptly decided that a Christian could not consistently keep slaves; but he did not dare to trust his own nature to determine the best manner of doing justice to those he had wronged. He therefore appointed a committee, before whom he laid a statement of the expenses he had incurred for the food and clothing of his slaves, and of the number of years, during which he had had the exclusive benefit of their labors. He conceived that he had no right to charge them for their freedom, because God had given them an inalienable right to that possession, from the very hour of their birth; but he wished the committee to decide what wages he ought to pay them for the work they had done. He cordially accepted the decision of the committee, paid the negroes their dues, and left them to choose such employments as they thought best. Many of the grateful slaves preferred to remain with him as hired laborers. It is hardly necessary to add that Moses Brown is a Quaker.

HIRED LABOR INSTEAD

It is commonly urged against emancipation that white men cannot possibly labor under the sultry climate of our most southerly States. This is a good reason for not sending the slaves out of the country, but it is no argument against making them free. No doubt we do need their labor; but we ought to pay for it. Why should their presence be any more disagreeable as hired laborers, than as slaves? In Boston, we continually meet colored people in the streets, and employ them in various ways, without being endangered, or even incommoded. There is no moral impossibility in a perfectly kind and just relation between the two races.

If white men think otherwise, let *them* remove from climates which nature has made too hot for their constitutions. Wealth or pleasure often induces men to change their abode; an emigration for the sake of humanity would be an agreeable novelty. Algernon Sidney said, "When I cannot live in my own country, but by such means as are worse than dying in it, I think God shows me that I ought to keep myself out of it."

But the slave holders try to stop all the efforts of benevolence, by vociferous complaints about infringing upon their *property;* and justice is so subordinate to self-interest, that the unrighteous claim is silently allowed, and even openly supported, by those who ought to blush for themselves, as Christians and as republicans. Let men *simplify* their arguments—let them confine themselves to one single question, "What right can a man have to compel his neighbor to toil without reward, and leave the same hopeless inheritance to his children, in order that *he* may live in luxury and indolence?" Let the doctrines of *expediency* return to the Father of Lies, who invented them, and gave them power to turn every way for evil. The Christian knows no appeal from the decisions of God, plainly uttered in his conscience. . . .

The personal liberty of one man can never be the property of another. All ideas of property are founded upon the mutual agreement of the human race, and are regulated by such laws as are deemed most conducive to the general good. In slavery there is no *mutual* agreement; for in that case it would not be slavery. The negro has no voice in the matter—no alternative is presented to him—no bargain is made. The beginning of his bondage is the triumph of power over weakness; its continuation is the tyranny of knowledge over ignorance. One man may as well claim an exclusive right to the air another man breathes, as to the possession of his limbs and faculties. Personal freedom is the birthright of every human being. God himself made it the first great law of creation; and no human enactment can render it null and void. . . .

Rights and Laws

Am I reminded that the *laws* acknowledge these vested rights in human flesh? I answer, the laws themselves were made by individuals, who wished to justify the wrong and profit by it. We ought never to have recognised a claim, which cannot exist according to the laws of God; it is our duty to atone for the error; and the sooner we make a beginning, the better will it be for us all. Must our arguments be based upon justice and mercy to the slave holders *only*? Have the negroes no right to ask compensation for their years and years of unrewarded toil? It is true that they have food and clothing, of such kind, and in such quantities, as their masters think proper. But it is evident that this is not the worth of their labor; for the proprietors can give from one hundred to five and six hundred dollars for a slave, beside the expense of supporting those who are too old or too young to labor. They could not *afford* to do this, if the slave did not earn more than he receives in food and clothing. If the laws allowed the slave to redeem himself progressively, the owner would receive his money back again; and the negro's years of uncompensated toil would be more than lawful interest.

The southerners are much in the habit of saying they really wish for emancipation, if it could be effected in safety; but I search in vain for any proof that these assertions are sincere. (When I say this, I speak collectively; there are, no doubt, individual exceptions.)

Instead of profiting by the experience of other nations, the slave owners, as a body, have resolutely shut their eyes against the light, because they preferred darkness. Every change in the laws has rivetted the chain closer and closer upon their victims; every attempt to make the voice of reason and benevolence heard has been overpowered with threatening and abuse. A cautious vigilance against improvement, a keen-eyed jealousy of all freedom of opinion, has characterized their movements. There *can* be no doubt that the *majority* wish to perpetuate slavery. They support it with loud bravado, or insidious sophistry, or pretended regret; but they never abandon the point. Their great desire is to keep the public mind turned in another direction. They are well aware that the ugly edifice is built of rotten timbers, and stands on slippery sands—if the loud voice of public opinion could be made to reverberate through its dreary chambers, the unsightly frame would fall, never to rise again.

Since so many of their own citizens admit that the polity of this system is unsound, and its effects injurious, it is wonderful that they do not begin to destroy the "costly iniquity" in good earnest. But long continued habit is very powerful; and in the habit of slavery are concentrated the strongest evils of human nature—vanity, pride, love of power, licentiousness, and indolence.

SOUTHERN MINORITY

There is a minority particularly in Virginia and Kentucky, who sincerely wish a change for the better; but they are overpowered, and have not even ventured to speak, except in the great Virginia debate of 1832. In the course of that debate the spirit of slavery showed itself without disguise. The members *talked* of emancipation; but with one or two exceptions, they merely wanted to emancipate or rather to send away, the *surplus* population, which they could neither keep nor sell, and which might prove dangerous. They wished to get rid of the consequences of the evil, but were determined to keep the evil itself. Some members from Western Virginia, who spoke in a better spirit, and founded their arguments on the broad principles of justice, not on the mere convenience of a certain class, were repelled with angry excitement. The eastern districts threatened to separate from the western, if the latter persisted in expressing opinions opposed to the continuance of slavery. From what I have uniformly heard of the comparative prosperity of Eastern and Western Virginia, I should think this was very much like the town's poor threatening to separate from the town.

The mere circumstance of daring to debate on the subject was loudly reprimanded; and there was a good deal of indignation expressed that "reckless editors, and imprudent corre-spondents, had presumed so far as to allude to it in the columns of a newspaper." Discussion in the Legislature was strongly deprecated until a plan had been formed; yet they must have known that no plan could be formed, in a republi-can government, without previous discussion. The proposal contained within itself that self-perpetuating power, for which the schemes of slave owners are so remarkable. . . .

SLAVERY CANNOT LAST

This state of things cannot last. The operations of Divine Providence are hastening the crisis, and move which way we will, it must come in some form or other; if we take warning in time, it may come as a blessing. The spirit of philanthropy . . . *is* walking to and fro in the earth; and it will not pause, or turn back, till it has fastened the golden band of love and peace around a sinful world.—The sun of knowledge and liberty is already high in the heavens—it is peeping into every dark nook and corner of the earth—and the African cannot be al-ways excluded from its beams.

The advocates of slavery remind me of a comparison I once heard differently applied: Even thus does a dog, unwill-ing to follow his master's carriage, bite the wheels, in a vain effort to stop its progress.

CHAPTER 3

THE NATION ERUPTS: THE 1850S AND 1860S

AMERICAN
SOCIAL
MOVEMENTS

Aggressive Abolition

STANLEY HARROLD

Stanley Harrold is a professor of history and of political science at South Carolina State University. Abolitionism is his field of study. The section that follows is taken from Harrold's book *American Abolitionists*. Here he traces the increasingly aggressive antislavery movement through the 1840s and 1850s. As politics of the time focused on compromise over the issue of slavery, abolitionists became more and more dissatisfied with concessions granted to slaveholders and proslavery advocates. To break up this state of affairs, abolitionists formed their own political factions and elected third-party officials to public office. As these men brought uncompromising antislavery platforms to government debate, other abolitionists engaged in more direct action. Some of these activists acted as legal defenders for slaves who had escaped to the North, while others aided runaway slaves along the Underground Railroad. All of these actions strained relations between the North and South and steered the nation toward civil war.

I n contrast to the American Anti-Slavery Society (AASS), the newer antislavery organizations actively promoted abolitionism in the South. Throughout its existence from 1840 until it was replaced by the American Abolition Society in 1855, the American and Foreign Anti-Slavery Society (AFASS) published antislavery propaganda for distribution in slaveholding regions and otherwise encouraged antislavery action in the South. The American Missionary Association (AMA) employed antislavery missionaries in the upper South. Liberty party factions initiated two distinct strategies for weakening slavery on its northern periphery.

The more aggressive abolitionism of the 1840s and 1850s was in part a product of developments within the antislavery movement. But it also came in response to increasing slave unrest and in the context of a broader struggle between the North and South over slavery and its expansion into the West.

THE PLOT TO EXPAND SLAVERY

The belief among northerners that southern politicians conspired to use their power within the United States government to extend slavery into new regions dated to the struggle over Missouri Territory's application for admission to the Union as a slaveholding state in 1819. The proposition that a territory located so far north could become a slave state raised a fierce reaction among northerners fearful that their section would be hemmed in by slaveholders and slaves. The crisis ended in 1820 with the passage of the Missouri Compromise that—while admitting Missouri as a slave state and admitting Maine as a free state—prohibited slavery in the rest of the existing United States territories north of the 36°31' line of latitude.

While most northerners were satisfied with this settlement, abolitionists during the 1830s further developed the idea that a 'slave power' conspiracy, dedicated to promoting the interests of slaveholders at the expense of nonslaveholders, was a permanent presence within the United States government. During the 1840s this concept transcended abolitionism and became common among northerners. One did not need to sympathize with the enslaved or seek racial justice to believe that a slaveholding aristocracy threatened northern prosperity, westward expansion of free white labor, freedom of speech, press, and petition, and democracy itself.

It was the annexation of the Mexican province of Texas to the United States as a slave state in 1845 that led to the proliferation of this outlook in the North. Antipathy to slaveholders intensified as President James K. Polk, a slaveholding Democrat from Tennessee, began in May 1846 a war aimed at securing for the United States an enlarged version of Texas and the huge Mexican provinces of California and New Mexico. As soon as this war against Mexico began, a minority of northern Whig politicians joined abolitionists to denounce it as part of a plot to expand slavery.

Then, in August 1846, northern Whig and Democratic members of Congress united to pass the Wilmot Proviso, which proposed to ban slavery in all territories gained as a result of the war. Although the Proviso never became law, it contributed—along with abolitionist threats to slavery in Washington, DC and other border regions—to a sectional crisis during the late 1840s. By that time, most white southerners were convinced that an abolitionist North aimed to destroy slavery and provoke race war.

The character and outcome of the presidential election of 1848 were especially disturbing to these southerners. That year both major parties had attempted to avoid the issue of the Wilmot Proviso. The Democrats nominated Lewis Cass of Michigan and advocated *popular sovereignty*—having settlers rather than Congress decide the status of slavery in each United States territory. The Whigs nominated slaveholding war hero Zachary Taylor of Louisiana, while remaining silent about slavery in the territories. This evasion led to the organization in the North of the Free Soil party, which opposed slavery expansion. Although most white southerners were relieved when Taylor won the election, they were soon disillusioned. As president, Taylor—who had fallen under the influence of northern Whig leader William H. Seward—insisted on admitting California as a free state without making concessions to the South.

Threats by southern leaders to take their states out of the Union unless Congress protected slaveholding interests led to the Compromise of 1850, which temporarily quieted discord between the North and South. The Compromise admitted California as a free state, applied popular sovereignty to New Mexico, and abolished the slave trade but not slavery in the District of Columbia. Most significant for abolitionists was the inclusion in the compromise measures of a new fugitive slave law. It came in response to rising slave escapes and fear among white southerners that abolitionist aid to such escapes was undermining slavery in the border South. The new law authorized federal marshals to assist masters in recapturing escaped slaves, denied jury trials to alleged fugitives, created special federal commissioners to hear cases, and made it a federal crime to help slaves escape.

SLAVE UNREST

In fact it was enslaved African Americans who encouraged northern abolitionists to be more aggressive against slavery in the South. Nat Turner left an impression among abolitionists that, despite racialist notions of black docility, there were black liberators in the South ready to strike for freedom. . . . Abolitionists perceived that slavery was vulnerable on its northern periphery and they developed strategies designed to exploit that vulnerability.

The revolt of enslaved West Africans on the Spanish schooner *Amistad* in 1839 had no direct connection with slavery in the border South. But it did introduce revolt leader Joseph Cinque as a black hero, set a precedent for abolitionist cooperation with slave rebels, and led to the organization of the AMA. Following the Africans' successful revolt, a United States warship captured the *Amistad* and carried the Africans to jail in New Haven, Connecticut. In response, Lewis Tappan initiated legal action that led to a Supreme Court decision freeing them in 1841. The AMA was a product of Tappan's successful effort to return the Africans to their homeland. . . .

THIRD-PARTY POLITICS

At the same time that abolitionists became more aware of slave unrest, a majority of them embraced third-party politics. The movement for what became the Liberty party began in western New York during the late 1830s. Myron Holley, Alvan Stewart, and other abolitionists in that region were disillusioned with moral suasion and efforts to abolitionize the northern wings of the Whig and Democratic parties. Because Democrats were rarely receptive to their appeals and because northern Whigs claimed to represent Christian morality and antislavery sentiment, most abolitionists had voted for Whig candidates. But as members of a national party, Whig politicians were unable to maintain consistent antislavery positions. They supported slaveholding candidates for the presidency and proslavery measures in Congress.

Abolitionists, the Liberty leaders contended, had to save themselves from this sinful complicity in upholding slavery by coming out of the existing parties just as they had come out of proslavery churches. But from the start political abolitionists also had more aggressive intentions. They aimed to transform politics in the North, carry antislavery principles into the South, and change the existing proslavery interpretation of the United States Constitution.

By April 1840, when they nominated James G. Birney—a reformed slaveholder—for president, the New Yorkers had been joined by political abolitionists in Massachusetts led by Joshua Leavitt and Henry B. Stanton. Shortly thereafter they gained the support of Ohio abolitionists led by Gamaliel Bailey and, by 1841, Salmon P. Chase.

Birney had no chance to garner a respectable third-party vote in 1840. This was because northern Whigs presented their presidential nominee, William Henry Harrison, as an antislavery candidate and argued that votes for Birney would help re-elect the incumbent proslavery Democratic president, Martin Van Buren. Out of a total of 2,411,187 popular votes cast, Birney received just 7,056. Birney did better as the Liberty presidential nominee in 1844. After four years of third-party organizing—chiefly in Massachusetts, Ohio, and New York—and a proliferation of Liberty newspapers, Birney received 65,608 votes out of a total of 2,871,906. . . .

LIBERTY PARTY AIMS

All Liberty abolitionists sought to agitate the moral issue of slavery within a political context. They all rejected Garrisonian nonresistance and the contention that the United States Constitution was proslavery. But the dominant Liberty leaders in New York and Ohio disagreed concerning the party's role in destroying slavery, while the Massachusetts faction ineffectively sought a middle course.

The New Yorkers are best described as radical political abolitionists. Led after 1840 by Gerrit Smith and including prominent black abolitionists such as Henry Highland Garnet and (later) Frederick Douglass, they subordinated conventional party politics to their interpretation of God's law and to direct action against slavery in the border South. They insisted that the United States Constitution, interpreted in accordance with the Bible and natural law, made slavery illegal throughout the United States. According to their reasoning, either Congress or the Supreme Court had power to abolish slavery in the southern states. More significantly, they maintained that since all laws recognizing slavery were unconstitutional, it was perfectly legal for slaves to escape and for abolitionists to aid them. As far as the radical political abolitionists were concerned, the most sincere abolitionists were those who dared to go south to put this precept into effect.

During the early 1840s, radical political abolitionists Gerrit Smith and Henry Highland Garnet rhetorically called on slaves actively to resist their masters. In January 1842, Smith urged slaves to steal what they needed to escape and urged northern abolitionists to go south to help them. In August 1843, at a Black National Convention meeting in Buffalo, Garnet advised slaves to stop working in order to force masters either to free them or to initiate a violent confrontation.

In contrast, the Ohio Liberty leaders distinguished between abolitionism as a moral struggle and the Liberty party as a conventional political organization. The party, Bailey and Chase maintained, was bound by the common interpretation of the United States Constitution, which recognized the legality of slavery in the states and the power of Congress over it within the national domain. The proper aims of the Liberty party, said Chase, were to *denationalize* slavery by abolishing it within Congress's jurisdiction, to withdraw all federal support for it within the southern states, and to form abolitionist parties in those states. The Ohio Liberty leaders opposed radical political abolitionist advocacy of United States government action against slavery in the South. They also opposed clandestine efforts to help slaves escape. The Ohioans rejected these tactics because they believed they would reduce the third-party vote in the North and prevent the spread of political abolitionism into the South.

Their incompatible views caused continuous strife between the New York and Ohio Liberty organizations. The New Yorkers charged that the Ohio party's Cincinnati leadership wished to free only white northerners from the slave power, claimed that the Cincinnatians disdained African Americans, and that they were callous toward fugitive slaves. Bailey responded that the radical political abolitionists hurt the antislavery cause by advocating illegal acts.

The two factions irrevocably separated during the late 1840s as opposition to the expansion of slavery into the territories made the Ohioans' demand for denationalization attractive to a minority of northern Democrats and Whigs. The Barnburner faction of the New York Democratic party as well as the Conscience Whigs of Massachusetts and Ohio had come to oppose slavery expansion and the dominance of slaveholders in the national government. While very few of these Democrats and Whigs were abolitionists, the chance to unite with them in a more powerful antislavery party was irresistible to most Liberty leaders. Therefore, after considerable soul searching, the great majority of Liberty abolitionists joined with them in 1848 to form the Free Soil party.

Particularly difficult for Liberty abolitionists to accept were the antiblack sentiments expressed by the Barnburners and the choice of Barnburner leader Martin Van Buren as the Free Soil candidate for president. But only a few joined the radical political abolitionists in flatly refusing to support the Free Soil party. Those few nominated Gerrit Smith for president in 1848 and under a variety of names—including Liberty and Radical Political Abolitionist—maintained for over a decade a minuscule but influential organization centered in western New York. Their more important efforts, however, continued to be devoted to destabilizing slavery in the upper South through aid to the enslaved.

This aid took a variety of forms, including assisting individuals who had been kidnapped into slavery, supporting freedom suits initiated by slaves, purchasing freedom, and helping slaves escape. Such undertakings weakened slavery in the border South by challenging the assumption that enslavement was the natural condition of African Americans. Aid to kidnapping victims, freedom suits, and attempts to purchase freedom aroused sympathy among whites and encouraged an antislavery morality. Assisted slave escapes directly undermined the slave system by encouraging panicky masters to sell their chattels south, which—as African Americans sought to protect themselves and their loved ones—in turn produced more purchases of freedom and escapes.

All of these forms of direct action against slavery predated radical political abolitionism. They originated among African Americans in the Chesapeake and, as early as the 1790s, attracted local white abolitionist support. But, as the domestic slave trade put more black families at risk of dismemberment, radical political abolitionist doctrines encouraged northerners to go south to aid them.

During the early 1840s, when the term 'underground railroad' first appeared in newspapers, abolitionists were divided concerning helping slaves escape. Bailey, Chase, and Cassius M. Clay feared that contacts with slaves undermined efforts to establish abolitionist parties in the South. Some Garrisonians supported helping slaves escape but rarely went South themselves; others deprecated spending scarce funds on 'the running off of slaves.' But black and white radical political abolitionists were united in insisting that such direct action would do more to free the slaves than either votes or windy speeches.

Underground railroading transcended radical political abolitionism and, even during the 1840s and 1850s, most slaves who escaped did so on their own. There never was a united underground railroad operation with a unified administration. But by the early 1840s there were organized, biracial efforts designed to help slaves escape along predetermined routes from the border South to Canada. . . .

Today the best remembered underground railroad agent is Harriet Tubman. But ... Tubman was not well known during the 1850s except among a few abolitionists and people she helped. Having herself escaped from slavery in Maryland in 1849, she returned as many as nineteen times to help others. . . . She depended on a network of black and white abolitionists for support. Her bravery and that of other African Americans helped complicate white abolitionist views of black character.

After a Garrisonian suggested that the underground railroad had little antislavery impact because it only went one way, Thomas Wentworth Higginson—a young white abolitionist who knew Tubman—replied, 'Year by year new track is being laid, and the cars are running back again—cars that take these heroic self-emancipated fugitives move heroically back from Canada into the midst of slavery again, that they may bring out their children and their friends with them.'

ON THE BORDER

Underground railroading exacerbated long-standing southern white fear of an alliance between northern abolitionists and slaves. This added to the difficulties faced by those who worked openly against slavery in the southern borderlands. Nevertheless, during the 1840s and 1850s, a few native-born southern whites and a few northern transplants promoted political action for either gradual or immediate abolition in Kentucky, Virginia, Maryland, and the District of Columbia. Their activities strengthened the impression among white southerners that slavery was under siege at its northern periphery.

Most of these individuals had ties to the Ohio or New York factions of the Liberty party. But Cassius M. Clay, who became the most famous of the southern abolitionists, had close ties to the Garrisonians as well. Born into a prominent slaveholding Kentucky family, Clay became an abolitionist after hearing Garrison speak at Yale College during the early 1830s. When, a decade later, Clay denounced slaveholders as sinners, rejected the colonization of former slaves in Africa, and established an antislavery newspaper in Lexington, he attracted the admiration of all northern abolitionists. Garrisonians presented him as proof of the positive impact on the South of their agitation and Ohio Liberty abolitionists sought to convert him from the Whig party.

Clay's propensity for ruthless violence and his enlistment to fight in the Mexican War in 1846 diminished northern abolitionist enthusiasm for him. But his daring emancipationist campaign for governor in 1851 and his continued emphasis of Christian morality and black rights restored his reputation. By the mid-1850s he was a leading figure in the radical antislavery wing of the Republican party.

While Clay had ties to all northern antislavery groups, most other southern political abolitionists were identified with just one or two. During the 1840s the tiny Liberty party in western Virginia operated as an adjunct to the Ohio party. By 1848, Clay's Kentucky friend and rival John G. Fee had gained the support of the AMA on behalf of his church-oriented antislavery efforts. In his political efforts, Fee aligned first with the Ohio Liberty abolitionists and by the mid-1850s had become a radical political abolitionist. Fee declared that slavery could never be legal and championed black rights. His associates helped slaves escape.

Another southern abolitionist with ties to the radical political abolitionists was John C. Underwood, a former New Yorker who operated about nineteen dairy farms in Virginia's Shenandoah Valley. In 1848, Underwood began employing free labor on those farms as a means of showing its superiority over slavery. He also hoped to attract other northern farmers who might serve as the core of an abolitionist party in Virginia. By the mid-1850s, Underwood, like Clay, had become a Republican. In 1856, slaveholders drove him out of Virginia in response to his public denunciation of slavery for its brutal oppression of African Americans.

The political abolitionists' most ambitious southern initiative, however, was the establishment in Washington, DC of the weekly *National Era,* which Bailey edited from 1847 until his death in 1859. A project initiated by the Liberty party and the AFASS, the *National Era* aimed to spread abolitionist sentiment throughout the South. Meanwhile its office served as the center of an antislavery lobbying effort in Congress.

Although the bulk of the newspaper's large circulation was in the North, it had readers in every southern state, which frightened slavery's supporters as much as its location in Washington. . . . Proslavery mobs attacked the paper's office three nights in a row and in 1850 southern congressmen established the *Southern Press* in an attempt to counter its influence.

Garrisonians and radical political abolitionists denounced Bailey, who successively supported the Liberty, Free Soil, and Republican parties, as only nominally abolitionist. But he retained the respect of local African Americans, who regarded him as one of their more trustworthy white allies in the border South. Neither Bailey nor any of the others who represented northern abolitionist values in the South should be confused with such southern colonizationists as Robert J. Breckinridge and Henry Clay of Kentucky or Hinton R. Helper of North Carolina, whose opposition to slavery was rooted almost exclusively in anti-black prejudice. . . .

THE ABOLITIONIST CHALLENGE

Slavery's defenders were aware that northern abolitionism had become more aggressive during the 1840s and 1850s. Prior to the Compromise of 1850, their denunciations of abolitionist interference in the border South vied with their objections to the Wilmot Proviso for predominance in their rhetoric. In several instances they portrayed aggressive abolitionism as the more significant of these threats, and they hoped that the new and stronger Fugitive Slave Law of 1850 would serve as a means of stopping abolitionist aid to escaping slaves. When the act proved ineffectual, they became even more fearful that the border South would soon be lost and that abolitionists would then move farther south.

Proslavery southerners could do little about abolitionists who remained in the North. But they could counter those brave men and women who ventured into the South to help slaves escape, advocate political abolitionism, establish anti-slavery churches, or build antislavery communities. Charles T. Torrey was not the only slave rescuer who faced prison and death. Cassius M. Clay and others who advocated abolitionist legislation had their newspaper presses destroyed and faced violence. Proslavery vigilantes repeatedly beat John G. Fee and his associates. There were similar assaults on Crooks and other Wesleyan missionaries in North Carolina and Virginia. Southern law enforcement officials arrested missionaries on charges that they helped slaves escape or incited them to insurrection.

Some abolitionists were more aggressive against slavery in the South than were others. But during the 1840s and 1850s virtually all of them were more willing than they had been during the 1830s to find ways of confronting slavery on its own ground. 'What we want, in my judgement, is not resistance to encroachment, but direct aggression,' Chase declared in 1846. Other abolitionists went beyond Chase's emphasis on formal political organization, and growing numbers of white southerners believed they had to act decisively to counter this abolitionist challenge.

Sectionalism in the 1850s

HENRY H. SIMMS

Henry H. Simms was an associate professor of history at Ohio State University when *A Decade of Sectional Controversy: 1851–1861* was first published in 1942. The piece that follows highlights the political tensions of the 1850s and how they were influenced by the abolitionist cause. Simms points out that politicians and other orators debated the issue of slavery so much that average Americans acquired unrealistic fears of how divided the nation was. Of course, these fears galvanized many segments of the population and actually led to the kind of extreme sectionalism that many believed was already widespread.

P olitical, psychological, constitutional and economic factors all played some part in producing the break between the sections and the war that followed. However, it seems to the writer that political and psychological factors played the paramount role in producing those unfortunate results. The extreme position taken by some of the public men in both sections of the country, particularly in overemphasizing the significance of the issue of slavery in the territories, no doubt strengthened those men politically in their respective sections, but led to unwarranted fears in the minds of many of their constituents. While many conservative voices were raised in both sections, there were altogether too many in both who indulged in extremes of criticism. That reciprocal abuse undoubtedly played considerable part in developing the emotional fervor which characterized the sectional controversy....

Political leaders, North and South, attached much significance to [the slavery] question. In the South it was frequently said that, if the group in the North trying to prohibit slavery in the territories should be successful, it would then assail the institution in the states. Alfred Iverson, a Senator from Georgia, felt that the Republican party, in order to live, would have to continue the war on slavery as long as the institution lasted. In dramatic fashion he declared that "The demon of abolition, in his most hideous form, has covered them [free states] all over with the footprints of his onward and remorseless march to power. . . . When the present Republican party, or its legitimate successor in some other name, shall get possession of the Government, when it has the President, both Houses of Congress, and the Judiciary, what will stay its hand? It cannot stand still; if it does, it dies. To live and reign, it must go on. Step by step it will be driven onward in its mad career until slavery is abolished or the Union dissolved. One of these two things is as inevitable as death." Lucius Quintus Cincinnatus Lamar, a representative in Congress from Mississippi, queried the Republicans in the following manner: "I ask you if you do not know that when you strike slavery from the Territories you have taken the initial and most decisive step toward the destruction of slavery in the States."

Jefferson Davis declared that the reason Southerners were concerned over slavery in the territories was "simply because of the war that is made against our institutions; simply because of the want of security which results from the action of our opponents in the Northern States. . . . You have made it a political war. We are on the defensive. How far are you to push us?" In a letter written in 1860, the Mississippi Senator expressed more emphatically his view that the Republicans were aiming to strike at slavery in the states. While certain expressions used from time to time by Republicans could be construed to mean a purpose to attack slavery in the states, yet that purpose was not stated in their party platforms, and their leaders, such as Lincoln, Wade and Chase, claimed that interference with the institution in the states was no part of their program.

The strong Southern defense of slavery against the vigorous assaults directed at the institution and the Dred Scott decision legalizing it in the territories were in large part made the bases of Northern claims that the South was trying to spread slavery all over the free states. Horace Mann declared in 1852 that, in looking for room to expand their institution, the slaveholders would try to extend it everywhere, until "even the free states" would be "engulfed with the rest, so that the dove of freedom will have no spot on the surface of the globe where she can set her foot." After the Dred Scott decision the *New York Tribune* warned New England of the impending "horror" of having the institution of slavery established there. . . .

Several books during the [1850s] tended, as a result of their extreme nature, to add fuel to the sectional flames. Mrs. Harriet Beecher Stowe's *Uncle Tom's Cabin*, published in 1852, may not, critically examined, have been as severe an indictment of Southern institutions as some represented it to be, but, since it portrayed dramatically the worst features of the slavery system, it is entirely probable that that large segment of the Northern public which read it and saw it acted at the theatres received a distorted impression of slavery in practice. Theatres were packed when the play was presented, and the book was read by hundreds of thousands soon after publication.

The book caused a sensation in the South. The *Richmond Dispatch* thought that Mrs. Stowe's reception in England, and the rejoicing in the North at that reception, had thrown "discredit" on the institutions and morals of the South. Extracts from the *New Orleans Picayune* afford a fair index as to the novel's reception in the slaveholding section. Commenting upon the fact that the work was to be put upon the stage, the *Picayune* said that it would be "acted by living libellers before crowds of deluded spectators." The South would be represented to the North "as living in a state of profligacy, cruelty and crime—tyrants who fear no God, and cruelly oppress their fellow creatures; and the drama is thus enlisted among the promoters of sectional hatred, a teacher and preacher of national discord, whose end inevitably would be the disruption of the Union.". . .

In the Northern press, the most severe indictment of the South that came to the attention of the author was found in the *New York Times,* a paper conservative in some ways. "Southern gentlemen" once existed, but they were a thing of the past. The Southerner had "become a money-getter and a mammon-worshiper." The expansion of slavery had made that institution "a mighty gambling house of the most simply sordid nature." Culture and breeding had declined to the point where the South could not handle her simplest economic problems, nor secure a professor for her wealthiest university, even when a large salary was offered. This state of things had made "the tone of the public press and of the public men of the South ... more and more vulgar, barbaric and indecent." "Vituperation" and "vile and foul" epithets were the order of the day. The North, however, had grown in resources, had made great cultural advance, and refinement of tone was characteristic of her press and public men. Almost a year after this comparison of the sections, that journal declared that the slaveholder had corrupted manners generally. His barbarism had crossed the Potomac, so that "We now-a-days in the sober North carry our pistols and knives, have our difficulties in the streets, butcher our men unawares in bar-rooms, and then fly to the police for refuge, just as our Southern confreres have been doing for half a century."

Near personal encounters and violent language in both the House and Senate early in 1860 illustrate the fanatical extremes to which some of the actors in the sectional drama went. Owen Lovejoy, of Illinois, in the House in menacing fashion, assailed both slavery and slaveholders. Slaveholding he characterized as "more criminal" than "piracy" or "robbery," as "the sum of all villainy. Put every crime perpetrated among men into a moral crucible, and dissolve and combine them all, and the resulting amalgam is slaveholding." The South was drifting into "barbarism," a tendency checked only by some pure Christian women already in the slave states, and by the "Christian women" who had gone from the free states, and married in the slave states. Doctrines uttered by Southerners would be a "disgrace anywhere outside the five points of hell and the Democratic party." The slaveholders, he charged, paid their "debts by raising the mad-dog cry of abolition against the agents of your creditors." Roger Pryor, of Virginia, advancing toward Lovejoy as the latter approached the Democratic side, accused him of using "insulting language," an accusation which drew from John F. Potter, of Wisconsin, the statement that the opponents of Lovejoy had been using "violent and offensive language" for eight weeks. William Barksdale, of Mississippi, called the Illinois Representative "a black hearted scoundrel and nigger-stealing thief," and O.R. Singleton, also from Mississippi, referred to him as "a mean, despicable wretch."....

On June 4, 1860, Charles Sumner entertained the Senate with a speech which made the one entitled "The Crime Against Kansas" seem mild. His subject in 1860 was "The Barbarism of Slavery," and in it slavery was characterized as follows: "Barbarous in origin, barbarous in law, barbarous in all its pretensions, barbarous in the instruments it employs, barbarous in consequences, barbarous in spirit, barbarous wherever it shows itself, slavery must breed Barbarians, while it develops everywhere, alike in the individual and the society to which he belongs, the essential elements of Barbarism." So brutal was the South that "assassination" was "lifted to be one of the Fine Arts," and the slavery on which Southerners lived, "in all its fivefold foulness, must become part of themselves, discoloring the very soul, blotting the character, and breaking forth in moral leprosy."

Senator Chesnut, of South Carolina, was the only Southern Senator to reply to Sumner. He said that Southerners were not "inclined again to send forth the recipient of punishment howling through the world, yelping fresh cries of slander and malice." Chesnut, however, did denounce the Massachusetts Senator in the following language: "In the heroic ages of the world men were deified for the possession and the exercise of some virtues—wisdom, truth, justice, magnanimity, courage. In Egypt, also, we know they deified beasts and reptiles; but even that bestial people worshipped their idols on account of some supposed virtue. It has been left for this day, for this country, for the abolitionists of Massachusetts to deify the incarnation of malice, mendacity and cowardice." Unhealthy emotional attitudes were the inevitable product of such utterances as those to be found in the preceding pages.

John Brown Was Right

W.E.B. Du Bois

W.E.B. Du Bois (1868–1961), the first African American to receive a Ph.D. from Harvard (1896), was an intellectual, a leader, and a founder of the NAACP (National Association for the Advancement of Colored People) in 1909. Du Bois's biography of John Brown first appeared in 1909 and reveals a favorable opinion of the controversial abolitionist. Brown was a jack-of-all-trades who believed with religious fervor that slavery was an evil institution that would have to be destroyed by force. He, along with several followers (including two of his own sons), staged a raid on the U.S. arsenal at Harpers Ferry in Virginia (now West Virginia). Their plan was to seize weapons and arm slaves along the border states, in hopes of inciting a slave rebellion. After capturing the arsenal, Brown and his group took sixty hostages, but no slaves came forth to help or take up arms. Once there, he was set upon by a detachment of the U.S. military. A gun battle ensued in which ten of Brown's men were killed, and Brown himself was captured. After a famous trial that enflamed the passions of abolitionists and proslavery advocates, Brown—still defiant and believing in the justness of his cause—was hanged for his crime. For Du Bois, John Brown's violent tactics were appropriate because slavery still had the implicit support of the government in 1859. In Du Bois's view, slavery would not have disappeared quietly but would have "to die by revolution" through the aggressive acts of men like John Brown.

At high noon on Tuesday, October 18th, the raid was over. John Brown lay wounded and bloodstained on the floor and the governor of Virginia bent over him.

"Who are you?" he asked.

Excerpted from *John Brown*, by W.E.B. Du Bois (New York: Kraus-Thompson Organization Limited, 1973).

"My name is John Brown; I have been well known as old John Brown of Kansas. Two of my sons were killed here to-day, and I'm dying too. I came here to liberate slaves, and was to receive no reward. I have acted from a sense of duty, and am content to await my fate; but I think the crowd have treated me badly. I am an old man. Yesterday I could have killed whom I chose; but I had no desire to kill any person, and would not have killed a man had they not tried to kill me and my men. I could have sacked and burned the town, but did not; I have treated the persons whom I took as hostages kindly, and I appeal to them for the truth of what I say. If I had succeeded in running off slaves this time, I could have raised twenty times as many men as I have now, for a similar expedition. But I have failed.". . .

THE RIDDLE OF THE SPHINX

The deed was done. The next day the world knew and the world sat in puzzled amazement. It was ever so and ever will be. When a prophet like John Brown appears, how must we of the world receive him? Must we follow out the drear, dread logic of surrounding facts, as did the South, even if they crucify a clean and pure soul, simply because consistent allegiance to our cherished, chosen ideal demands it? If we do, the shame will brand our latest history. Shall we hesitate and waver before his clear white logic, now helping, now fearing to help, now believing, now doubting? Yes, this we must do so long as the doubt and hesitation are genuine; but we must not lie. If we are human, we must thus hesitate until we know the right. How shall we know it? That is the Riddle of the Sphinx. We are but darkened groping souls, that know not light often because of its very blinding radiance. Only in time is truth revealed. To-day at last we know: John Brown was right.

Yet there are some great principles to guide us. That there are in this world matters of vast human import which are eternally right or eternally wrong, all men believe. Whether that great right comes, as the simpler, clearer minded think, from the spoken word of God, or whether it is simply another way of saying: this deed makes for the good of mankind, or that, for the ill—however it may be, all men know that there are in this world here and there and again and again great partings of the ways—the one way wrong, the other right, in some vast and eternal sense. This certainly is true at times—in the mighty crises of lives and nations. On the other hand, it is also true, as human experience again and again shows, that the usual matters of human debate and difference of opinion are not so vitally important, or so easily classified; that in most cases there is much of right and wrong on both sides and, so usual is it to find this true, that men tend to argue it always so. Their life morality becomes always a wavering path of expediency, not necessarily the best or the worst path, as they freely even smilingly admit, but a good path, a safe path, a path of little resistance and one that leads to the good if not to the theoretical (but usually impracticable) best. Such philosophy of the world's ways is common, and probably it is well that thus it is. And yet we all feel its temporary, tentative character; we instinctively distrust its comfortable tone, and listen almost fearfully for the greater voice; its better is often so far below that which we feel is a possible best, that its present temporizing seems evil to us, and ever and again after the world has complacently dodged and compromised with, and skilfully evaded a great evil, there shines, suddenly, a great white light—an unwavering, unflickering brightness, blinding by its all-seeing brilliance, making the whole world simply a light and a darkness—a right and a wrong. Then men tremble and writhe and waver. They whisper, "But—but—of course;" " the thing is plain, but it is too plain to be true—it is true but truth is not the only thing in the world." Thus they hide from the light, they burrow and grovel, and yet ever in, and through, and on them blazes that mighty light with its horror of darkness and behind it peals the voice—the Riddle of the Sphinx, that must be answered.

Such a light was the soul of John Brown. He was simple, exasperatingly simple; unlettered, plain, and homely. No casuistry of culture or of learning, of well-being or tradition moved him in the slightest degree: "Slavery is wrong," he said,—"kill it."

Destroy it—uproot it, stem, blossom, and branch; give it no quarter, exterminate it and do it now. Was he wrong? No. The forcible staying of human uplift by barriers of law, and might, and tradition is the most wicked thing on earth. It is wrong, eternally wrong. It is wrong, by whatever name it is called, or in whatever guise it lurks, and whenever it appears. But it is especially heinous, black, and cruel when it masquerades in the robes of law and justice and patriotism. So was American slavery clothed in 1859, and it had to die by revolution, not by milder means. And this men knew. They had known it a hundred years. Yet they shrank and trembled. From round about the white and blinding path of this soul flew equivocations, lies, thievings and red murders. And yet all men instinctively felt that these things were not of the light but of the surrounding darkness. It is at once surprising, baffling and pitiable to see the way in which men—honest American citizens—faced this light. Many types met and answered the argument, John Brown (for he did not use argument, he was himself an argument). First there was the Western American—the typical American, like Charles Robinson—one to whose imagination the empire of the vale of the Mississippi appealed with tremendous force. Then there was the Abolitionist—shading away from him who held slavery an incubus to him who saw its sin, of whom Gerrit Smith was a fair type. Then there was the lover of men, like Dr. Howe, and the merchant-errant like [George] Stearns. Finally, there were the two great fateful types—the master and the slave.

To Robinson, Brown was simply a means to an end—beyond that he was whatever prevailing public opinion indicated. When the gratitude of Osawatomie [the Kansas settlement where Brown's gang was formed] swelled high, Brown was fit to be named with Jesus Christ; when the wave of Southern reaction subjugated the nation, he was something less than a fanatic. But whatever he was, he was the sword on which struggling Kansas and its leaders could depend, the untarnished doer of its darker deeds, when they that knew them necessary cowered and held their hands. Brown's was not the only hand that freed Kansas, but his hand was indispensable, and not the first time, nor the last, has a cool and skilful politician, like Robinson, climbed to power on the heads of those helpers of his, whose half realized ideals he bartered for present possibilities—human freedom for statehood. For the Abolitionist of the Garrison type Brown had a contempt, as undeserved as it was natural to his genius. To recognize an evil and not strike it was to John Brown sinful. "Talk, talk, talk," he said derisively. Nor did he rightly gauge the value of spiritual as contrasted with physical blows, until the day when he himself struck the greatest on the Charleston scaffold.

BROWN AMONG OTHER ABOLITIONISTS

But if John Brown failed rightly to gauge the movement of the Abolitionists, few of them failed to appreciate him when they met him. Instinctively they knew him as one who grasped the very pith and kernel of the evil which they fought. They asked no proofs or credentials; they asked John Brown. So it was with Gerrit Smith. He saw Brown and believed in him. He entertained him at his house. He heard his detailed plans for striking slavery a heart blow. He gave him in all over a thousand dollars, and bade him Godspeed! Yet when the blow was struck, he was filled with immeasurable consternation. He equivocated and even denied knowledge of Brown's plans. To be sure, he, his family, his fortune were in the shadow of danger—but where was John Brown? So with Dr. Howe, whose memory was painfully poor on the witness stand and who fluttered from enthusiastic support of Brown to a weak wavering when once he had tasted the famous Southern hospitality. He found slavery, to his own intense surprise, human: not ideally and horribly devilish, but only humanly bad. Was a bad human institution to be attacked *vi et armis?* [by force of arms] Or was it not rather to be met with persuasive argument in the soft shade of a Carolina veranda? Dr. Howe inclined to the latter thought, after his Cuban visit, and he was exceedingly annoyed and scared after the raid. He fled precipitately to Canada. Of the Boston committee only Stearns stood up and out in the public glare and said un-equivocally, then and there: "I believe John Brown to be the representative man of this century, as Washington was of the last—the Harpers Ferry affair, and the capacity shown by the Italians for self-government, the great events of this age. One will free Europe and the other America."

Antislavery and the Republican Party

JOHN B. ALLEY

In the face of sectionalism, a new Republican party emerged in the 1850s. On April 30, 1860, the Honorable John B. Alley of Massachusetts delivered a speech entitled "Principles and Purposes of the Republican Party" in the House of Representatives. Alley's speech, given prior to the Republican Convention in this presidential election year, outlines the highly sectional goals of the party. Expressing confidence in the Republicans' ability to place its yet-to-be-determined candidate in the White House, Alley underscores the importance of curtailing the expansion of slavery in the party's platform for the coming election. In addition to strong antislavery sentiment, Alley's speech foretells the South's bid for disunion and insists that the Republicans will do all within their power to preserve the nation.

Mr. Chairman, in the remarks which I shall submit to the consideration of the committee at this time, I propose to discuss the principles and purposes of the Republican party, the causes which led to, and the necessity of its organization, the inevitable tendency of its doctrines, and the final result of its action.

Slavery has been, to a greater or less extent, a disturbing element in our national politics ever since the organization of the Government; in fact, political differences were occasioned by it, and sectional prejudices grew out of it, at a period long anterior to the formation of the Federal compact. . . .

The almost universal sentiment of the North is, that slavery is a great moral, social, and political evil; productive of no good, but much of evil to the master, as well as to the slave;

Excerpted from John B. Alley's speech "Principles and Purposes of the Republican Party," to the U.S. House of Representatives, April 30, 1860.

and to hold him as a chattel is in violation of every precept of Christianity, of every axiom of liberty, of every sentiment of justice, of every feeling of humanity. While they hold it to be a duty to oppose its further extension, they do not regard themselves as politically responsible for its existence and perpetuity in the States. So long as many of the most enlightened and gifted men of the South, who were statesmen and patriots, regarded it as an evil, and deplored its existence, and agreed with the North that it ought not to be extended, and declared, also, that it could not be defended upon any other ground than that of uncontrollable necessity, the North were satisfied to be quiet and content. But when it was discovered that it was the determined purpose of the South, in violation of all law and precedent, to force slavery everywhere, the people of the North became aroused, and now stand ready, with a unanimity proportioned to their conviction of the purposes and designs of the South, to declare "thus far, but no further"—not another inch of slave territory.

Upon this question of the extension of slavery, the South has been gradually growing desperate; until now it openly announces its treasonable purpose to dissolve this Union, if not permitted to use the whole force of this government to extend and protect slavery in all the national Territories. Many far seeing and sagacious people at the North have predicted for a long time this design of the South, but were unable to make the mass of the people believe it. But "whom the gods wish to destroy, they first make mad." The South have proclaimed it in unmistakable language; and the anti-slavery sentiment of the country will now take possession of the national Government. It cannot be averted. The South may rave and howl as much as it pleases; it must be done; and let me say to the South, these chosen Republican leaders will so administer the Government that every interest will be protected; that exact and equal justice will be done to the North as well as to the South, to the East and to the West. I am sorry to see, on the part of some, a disposition to apologize for the position and action of the Republican party, and claiming that the organization is a purely defensive one. It is well enough to state, what is the fact, that had it not been for the madness of the South upon this question, the Republican party would never have obtained its present gigantic proportions. But this party needs no apology. . . .

REPUBLICAN CONFIDENCE

The Republican party reflects every shade of opinion upon the question of slavery. The organization contains within its limits the most ultra conservative men, and the most zealous anti-slavery advocates, agreeing only upon one object, namely, the determination to prevent further extension of slavery.

The Democratic party contains within its folds the rankest secessionists or disunionists and the mildest conservatives, but all equally bent, at least so far as the organization is concerned, upon extending and perpetuating human slavery. But neither of the extremes of these two wings is destined to be immediately successful in obtaining possession of the national Government. The disunionists of the South could no more succeed in placing a representative of their ideas in the Presidential chair than the Abolitionists of the North can elect one of their number to that high position. But the anti-slavery sentiment of the North is thoroughly aroused; and, acting in conjunction with the conservatism of the whole country, it will place in the Presidential chair, on the 4th of March, 1861, a Republican President of conservative tendencies, but firm convictions; and . . . he will be sustained by the whole people of the North and the patriotic men of the South. You may as well make up your mind to it; you must submit to it.

These threats of dissolution of the Union are as the idle wind. The great body of the people at the South are not so deficient in understanding and intelligence as not to know that they could not live a moment, and maintain "their peculiar institution," outside of the Union, in hostility to the North. I have no fear of any serious movement for dissolution on the part of the South. "Barking dogs never bite." I confess I have some fears of the North, although I know they are a magnanimous and forbearing people; yet multitudes are beginning to feel that there is a point beyond which "forbearance ceases to be a virtue." When they consider that their commercial, their manufacturing, and all their political interests, are neglected and sacrificed, and everything made subservient to the interests of slavery, as they have been for years past; I say, when all this is fully realized, as it soon must be, it is impossible to predict what the consequences will be. Certain it is, that, first of all, they will rise in their might and demand their rights under the Constitution and laws. But let me tell gentlemen of the South, this Union will never be dissolved by them; it will take a mightier arm than theirs to overthrow this Government. If dissolved at all, it will be by the resistless will of the North.

Civil War and Emancipation

HERBERT APTHEKER

Herbert Aptheker is the author of a number of works on black history, specializing on the writings of W.E.B. Du Bois. When *Abolitionism: A Revolutionary Movement* was published in 1989, he was a professor at the University of California–Berkeley's law school. In the section that follows, Aptheker stresses the revolutionary character of the antislavery movement. The Civil War, in his view, was the culmination of the abolition movement's progressive efforts to remake the nation into a land of freedom for all people. In this context, the author discusses the Emancipation Proclamation and the Thirteenth Amendment, what each did and did not achieve, and how both were evidence of a government-sponsored declaration that the country's future greatness relied on the elimination of slavery and the expansion of rights and liberties to all Americans.

The antislavery agitation of the Abolitionists became more reasonable to increasing numbers of people in the pre–Civil War generation as the . . . socioeconomic transformation of the North proceeded. The platform of the Republican party—at its creation—reflected the transformation, which was characterized by a split in the mercantile bourgeoisie and banking interests as more and more of each serviced a free-labor economy rather than a slave-based one; the growth of an industrial bourgeoisie with needs—such as protective tariff, vast transportation networks, the populating of the West—that distinguished it from the planter class; and the growth of a working-class and free-farming population, which intensified the antislavery politics of a northern population of "greasy mechanics and filthy operatives" and "small-fisted farmers," as some southerners saw them. Added to these pressures upon the slave owners was the fourth development, the growing unrest of the southern slave population and the intensified class consciousness of an increasingly politicized nonslaveholding white population.

Faced with all these developments, the slaveholding oligarchy decided it had nothing to lose and everything to gain by taking up arms against opposing forces, if necessary, and establishing its own empire. When the oligarchy created its Confederacy—abstaining from submitting the question of secession to a popular vote until after the decision had been made at Montgomery [Alabama]—it made certain to give slavery top priority in its Constitution. By its terms, impairing private property rights in slaves was explicitly forbidden to the Confederate Congress. The Confederacy's vice president, Alexander H. Stephens of Georgia, explained in 1861, as we have seen, that slavery was fundamental to the Confederacy as was racism. He projected also that that institution would yet dominate the entire North American continent.

ANTISLAVERY ISSUES IN THE CIVIL WAR

There were four components to the revolutionary character of the Civil War; all were basically tied to the status of the Afro-American population and thus related to the meaning of Abolitionism. First, there was the question of the actual condition of the black people; this also entailed what the nature of the postwar South would be. Second was the question of remaking the nature of the Union as part of the process of successfully defending it. Third was the question of preserving a government based on the consent of the governed, on equality of rights, on due process of law, of popular sovereignty "of the People, by the People and for the People," with "People" becoming an increasingly all-inclusive concept. Fourth, as a necessary corollary of the third, was the question of amending the Constitution that would entail the most revolutionary changes in social conditions and property relations undertaken anywhere in the nineteenth century.

Since slavery was at the root of the Confederate effort, the undoing of slavery was at the heart of defeating the Confederacy. Slavery's existence had disrupted the Union; slavery's termination was necessary to save it. The reasons for this were manifold and interrelated: (1) a basic source of the Confederacy's strength lay in the labor of the slaves—free the slaves and that source vanished; (2) the black people wanted to fight, work for, and in all possible ways serve the Union—hence, they promised great (indispensable, Lincoln declared in 1864) strength to the Union effort; and (3) a Union policy of emancipation would bring enormous diplomatic advantage to Lincoln's government throughout Europe. . . .

MOVING TOWARD EMANCIPATION

1862 saw a proliferation of acts tending toward a policy of emancipation, culminating in the issuance, as of 1 January 1863, of the final Emancipation Proclamation. In February, a law was enacted forbidding all U.S. army officers from returning fugitive slaves to their masters. In March, President Lincoln formally submitted to Congress his suggestion that it resolve to help any state that adopted a plan for gradual emancipation with compensation. Congress promptly so resolved, but border-state representatives rejected the proposal. Nevertheless, London sources reported to the White House that this effort had a positive impact upon British public opinion.

On 10 April, Lincoln returned to his proposal of the preceding December, favoring gradual emancipation by individual states, with compensation to such states, but again the congressional delegations from the border states expressed opposition. Six days later a law was passed emancipating at once all slaves in the District of Columbia, with loyal slaveowners receiving $300 per slave. The law carried with it an appropriation of $100,000 for the voluntary colonization of those black people who wished to leave the United States.

Such proposals and efforts by government agencies in the past had always provoked expressions of disapproval from most

Afro-Americans; they had never resulted in any appreciable migration. This proposal met with the same result. When Lincoln became aware of widespread opposition to the latest colonization proposal, he took an unprecedented action: he invited a delegation of black people for an exchange of views on the question. Following this came mass meetings and published arguments from blacks rejecting the concept of colonization as flowing out of prejudice, as a hallmark of the slave system, as impractical, as immoral, and as contrary to the real interests of the United States. Rather than colonization, said an "Appeal from the Colored Men of Philadelphia": "We believe that the world would be benefited by giving the four millions of slaves their freedom, and the lands now possessed by their masters. They have been amply compensated in our labor and the blood of our kinsmen."

On 19 June, *Dred Scott* was put to rest when a law was passed abolishing slavery, without compensation, in all the federal territories. Also in June, ministers were appointed to Haiti and Liberia.

In July, perhaps inspired by the anniversary of the Declaration of Independence, Congress authorized the president to "employ persons of African descent for the suppression of the rebellion, and organize and use them in such manner as he may judge best for the public welfare." Although this did not specifically mention service as soldiers, the language certainly did not rule this out. The authorization was, in fact, the root of the policy that eventuated in over 180,000 black soldiers and some 25,000 black sailors as components of Lincoln's army and navy. . . .

LINCOLN AND THE UNION'S PRESERVATION

It was in July 1862 that Lincoln solicited the opinions of his cabinet members as to the wisdom of an emancipation announcement. The response was markedly cool; the least hostile suggested postponement until a notable military victory. Publicly, through the summer of 1862, Lincoln maintained his stance that the major purpose of the war was to preserve the

Union, not alter the status of slaves. But in fact the argument of Abolitionists, black and white, that saving the Union required emancipation (and that only a victorious Union would mean emancipation) became more and more persuasive as the war dragged on, casualties among whites mounted, and an absence of an emancipation policy embarrassed U.S. ministers abroad and enhanced the efforts of Confederate emissaries.

On 22 September 1862 was issued the Preliminary Emancipation Proclamation. Here the president took the nearly final step in transforming the war for the Union into a war for freedom, also. Still it gave the rebellious states, and portions thereof—to which alone it applied—one hundred days to stop the fighting and rejoin the nation; if they had not done so at the end of that period, irrevocable emancipation would be announced. Now, too, as he had done several times previously, Lincoln reiterated his preference for gradual, compensated emancipation.

[William Lloyd] Garrison had written and circulated a petition for emancipation that also called for compensating loyal owners. Black Abolitionists never put forth such proposals. Ralph Waldo Emerson on the announcement, 1 January 1863, of the final proclamation, included this stanza in his "Boston Hymn":

> Pay ransom to the owner,
> And fill the bag to the rim.
> Who is the owner? The slave is the owner,
> And ever was. *Pay him!*

The slave owners, however, remained adamant, and Lincoln issued his final Emancipation Proclamation. This act of confiscation was justified by Lincoln's designating that the proclamation was issued "by virtue of the power in me vested as Commander-in-Chief of the Army and Navy of the United States in time of actual armed rebellion." Lincoln here directed the armed forces of the United States to "maintain the freedom" of persons covered by the proclamation, and—contrary to the provision in the Constitution pledging the nation's military might to suppressing insurrections when requested by states to do so—they here were ordered to "do no act or acts to repress such persons, or any of them in any efforts they may make for their actual freedom." The proclamation expressed the hope that the people now "declared to be free" would "abstain from all violence, *unless in necessary self-defense*" (italics added)—which was much like the position of Henry Highland Garnet and John Brown.

Further, the freed people were urged, where possible, to "labor faithfully for reasonable wages." The proclamation added that persons freed by its provisions, if they were in "suitable condition," would be welcomed into the army "to garrison forts, positions, stations, and other places" and into the navy for all forms of service.

Although Lincoln closed by again citing "military necessity" as warranting the proclamation, he also announced that he "sincerely believed [it] to be an act of justice" for which he felt free to "invoke the considerate judgment of mankind and the gracious favor of Almighty God."

Lincoln's invoking of "the considerate judgment of mankind" reflected no mere rhetorical turn. In the first place, he despised slavery and was delighted to be able to deal it a death blow; in the second place, he knew that vehement opposition to emancipation was by no means absent in the North. Illustrating this latter fact was the resolution adopted by the Illinois State Legislature, whose majority was Democratic. It called the proclamation "a gigantic usurpation," which subverted the Union and constituted "a revolution in the social organization of the Southern States." This description, while troubling these Confederate sympathizers, accurately described the thrust of the proclamation.

It is likely that the proclamation, altering the previously announced purpose of the war, as a war for the Union, into one for a Free Union, provoked some public opposition in the North; certainly it was used to stimulate fearful antiblack—and antidraft—uprisings in several cities, notably New York and Detroit. But on the whole, its impact upon the war from a practical standpoint, let alone a moral one, was positive. By the end of 1862, public opinion in the North had been swung to a considerable degree to an antislavery, if not an Abolitionist, position. Figures like [Wendell] Phillips, Garrison, [Harriet Beecher] Stowe, and [Frederick] Douglass had become genuine mass leaders, listened to not by hundreds or thousands, as in the previous generation, but by millions. It certainly inspired the Afro-American population, free and slave, North and South; and it exerted indubitably a positive force upon mass public opinion abroad, not only in Europe, but also in Canada.

EFFECTS OF THE PROCLAMATION

The issuance of the proclamation was one of the great dramatic moments in history, eagerly awaited and fervently prayed for by millions for generations. It was an electric moment for them and for their allies. It was, of course, one of the great blows struck for human freedom in all history; it was also, as W.E.B. Du Bois first saw, a historic watershed in the history of working people. Chattel slavery had been dealt a mortal blow: the dignity of all labor had been enhanced; a divisive force in the working class had been lessened; the Bourbon concept that slavery was the proper condition of workers in general had been repudiated; the popular, democratic, essence of the struggle—the "People's War" feature, to quote Lincoln—had been vindicated.

Two immediate results of the proclamation appeared: one was the intensification of the recruitment of blacks for the armed forces of the Union; another was a strong impulse toward further development of the revolutionary quality of the war both in terms of permanently eliminating slavery throughout the nation and improving the status and condition of the Afro-American population.

When news of the proclamation reached the ears of the slaves, tens of thousands acted upon its promise and fled to Union forces. The turmoil, the inevitable antislavery content of the war, and, climactically, the proclamation induced what Du Bois in his *Black Reconstruction* had referred to as a "mobile General Strike."

Black enlistments and recruitment efforts brought over

200,000 black men, with about the same number of black men and women serving the Union forces as fortification builders, draymen, pilots, nurses, cooks, and so on. Because, at first, black soldiers were paid significantly less than white enlisted men, some (the Fifty-fourth and Fifty-fifth Massachusetts Regiments) refused all pay. They stayed with this "work action," until, finally, pay was at first equalized and then in the last months of the war equalized retroactively to the date of enlistment. On land and sea, the black men acquitted themselves very well; testimony to this effect by white officers (there were almost no black officers) seems to have been unanimous. Although black fighters faced especially onerous conditions and duties—they usually were less well equipped, longer on the line, and treated, originally, as insurrectionists rather than war prisoners if taken in combat—they contributed decisively to the victory of Lincoln's forces and therefore to the salvation of the Republic and their own liberation.

Following the issuance of the Emancipation Proclamation, the Abolitionists demanded (1) an immediate termination of slavery in the border states, wherein the proclamation did not apply; (2) the organization of a Freedmen's Bureau to guard the rights and interests of the newly freed people; and (3) the provision, through federal legislation and administration, of properly compensated labor to the freed people, of education for both adults and children, and of land to the tillers, to be either confiscated from or appropriated with compensation from the former major slave owners. Black groups and organizations emphasized in particular the land issue—for "he who owns the land owns the man"; the individuals like Sumner, Thaddeus Stevens, Wendell Phillips, Frederick Douglass, and Lydia Maria Child repeatedly stressed the basic significance of land distribution. Douglass pioneered in emphasizing early on the black man's need as well for three boxes—the ballot box, the jury box, and the cartridge box—or the suffrage, a nonracist judicial system, and a nonracist militia system. Much of this did not come to pass—a matter central to the history of the Reconstruction Era. Nevertheless, these demands were part of the context within which were debated the Civil War amendments, especially the Thirteenth. . . .

THE THIRTEENTH AMENDMENT

Slavery had been dealt devastating blows with the final Emancipation Proclamation and the flight from bondage of thousands of slaves. Then late in 1864 and early in 1865 Maryland and Missouri abolished slavery immediately and without compensation. But the culminating event was the passage, on 31 January 1865, of the Thirteenth Amendment by the necessary two-thirds vote of the House of Representatives.

Appropriate mass meetings heralding the passage were widely held in the North. At one such, in Boston on 4 February, Garrison was the featured speaker. Hailing the event with exultant enthusiasm, Garrison declared it had "constitutionalized" the Declaration of Independence; it had made that revolutionary manifesto "the supreme law of the land," its purpose being, he said, "the protection of the rights and liberties of all who dwell in the American soil."

On the face of it, the "protection of the rights and liberties" of all in the United States was the meaning of the Thirteenth Amendment, ratified by twenty-seven states, including eight of those that had been part of the Confederacy. The date of ratification was 6 December 1865. Its text was brief, unambiguous, unequivocal: "Neither slavery nor involuntary servitude, except as a punishment for crime whereof the party shall have been duly convicted, shall exist within the United States, or any place subject to their jurisdiction." This language was a vindication of the arguments of leading Abolitionists—like Theodore D. Weld, Lysander Spooner, William Goodell, and others—who had held that slavery had no legal existence in the United States since those held therein had never been charged or convicted of any crime and therefore were being denied their freedom—a "natural right" of all human beings—without due process of law. That argument was so well known to those who drafted the Thirteenth Amendment that it challenges credulity to believe there was no relationship between the two.

With the passage of the amendment, what then was the legal condition of the Afro-American freed people? That condition could be nothing other than *citizenship*. One draws this conclusion the more readily when recalling that the attorney general of the United States, Edward Bates, affirmed in November 1862 that free persons of color were citizens of the United States—thus contradicting [Supreme Court Justice Roger B.] Taney's opinion in *Dred Scott*. Further, the act establishing the Freedmen's Bureau on 3 March 1865 stated in its Section 4 that authority was herewith given to "set apart" abandoned land in the insurrectionary states, title to which was obtained by the United States, to a total of "not more than forty acres, to every male *citizen,* whether [loyal] refugee or freedman" (italics added).

Prior to the coming into force of the Thirteenth Amendment, several southern states—under Johnsonian restoration—had passed so-called Black Codes that went as far as ingenuity allowed to reinstate involuntary servitude without quite instituting chattel slavery. These codes, such as those of Mississippi and Louisiana, instituted peonage for the black population. Given these as instructive illustrations of what might replace slavery, the Thirteenth Amendment outlawed both slavery and involuntary servitude.

The Emancipation Proclamation

ABRAHAM LINCOLN

The Emancipation Proclamation was issued by President Lincoln on September 22, 1862, shortly after the Union army's victory at Antietam. The proclamation stated that as of January 1, 1863, slaves in southern states still in active rebellion were no longer bound to their masters. However, since the South was still in control of its territories, the proclamation had no immediate effect on those in bondage other than to raise their hopes of future freedom. What Lincoln's speech did do was to signify to both the North and South that putting an end to slavery had become a war aim of the federal government.

Whereas on the 22nd day of September, A.D. 1862, a proclamation was issued by the President of the United States, containing, among other things, the following, to wit:

"That on the 1st day of January, A.D. 1863, all persons held as slaves within any State or designated part of a State the people whereof shall then be in rebellion against the United States shall be then, thenceforward, and forever free; and the executive government of the United States, including the military and naval authority thereof, will recognize and maintain the freedom of such persons and will do no act or acts to repress such persons, or any of them, in any efforts they may make for their actual freedom.

"That the executive will on the 1st day of January aforesaid, by proclamation, designate the States and parts of States, if any, in which the people thereof, respectively, shall then be in rebellion against the United States; and the fact that any

Excerpted from Abraham Lincoln's speech "The Emancipation Proclamation," September 22, 1862.

State or the people thereof shall on that day be in good faith represented in the Congress of the United States by members chosen thereto at elections wherein a majority of the qualified voters of such States shall have participated shall, in the absence of strong countervailing testimony, be deemed conclusive evidence that such State and the people thereof are not then in rebellion against the United States."

Now, therefore, I, Abraham Lincoln, President of the United States, by virtue of the power in me vested as Commander-In-Chief of the Army and Navy of the United States in time of actual armed rebellion against the authority and government of the United States, and as a fit and necessary war measure for suppressing said rebellion, do, on this 1st day of January, A.D. 1863, and in accordance with my purpose so to do, publicly proclaimed for the full period of one hundred days from the first day above mentioned, order and designate as the States and parts of States wherein the people thereof, respectively, are this day in rebellion against the United States the following, to wit:

Arkansas, Texas, Louisiana (except the parishes of St. Bernard, Palquemines, Jefferson, St. John, St. Charles, St. James, Ascension, Assumption, Terrebone, Lafourche, St. Mary, St. Martin, and Orleans, including the city of New Orleans), Mississippi, Alabama, Florida, Georgia, South Carolina, North Carolina, and Virginia (except the forty-eight counties designated as West Virginia, and also the counties of Berkeley, Accomac, Morthhampton, Elizabeth City, York, Princess Anne, and Norfolk, including the cities of Norfolk and Portsmouth), and which excepted parts are for the present left precisely as if this proclamation were not issued.

And by virtue of the power and for the purpose aforesaid, I do order and declare that all persons held as slaves within said designated States and parts of States are, and henceforward shall be, free; and that the Executive Government of the United States, including the military and naval authorities thereof, will recognize and maintain the freedom of said persons.

And I hereby enjoin upon the people so declared to be free

to abstain from all violence, unless in necessary self-defence; and I recommend to them that, in all cases when allowed, they labor faithfully for reasonable wages.

And I further declare and make known that such persons of suitable condition will be received into the armed service of the United States to garrison forts, positions, stations, and other places, and to man vessels of all sorts in said service.

And upon this act, sincerely believed to be an act of justice, warranted by the Constitution upon military necessity, I invoke the considerate judgment of mankind and the gracious favor of Almighty God.

At Long Last, Emancipation

JOHN GREENLEAF WHITTIER

John Greenleaf Whittier's (1807–1892) work as a Quaker abolitionist is often overshadowed by his literary fame. He was a poet, editor, and essayist. In this 1863 letter to his friend William Lloyd Garrison, Whittier briefly reminisces over the passage of thirty years
since the founding of the American Anti-Slavery Society. Writing
shortly after the Emancipation Proclamation took effect, he expresses
his joy and relief that the end of slavery is at hand.

My Dear Friend: I have received thy kind letter with the
accompanying circular, inviting me to attend the commemoration of the Thirtieth Anniversary of the formation of
the American Anti-Slavery Society, at Philadelphia. It is with
the deepest regret that I am compelled, by the feeble state of
my health, to give up all hope of meeting thee and my other
old and dear friends on an occasion of so much interest. How
much it costs me to acquiesce in the hard necessity, thy own
feelings will tell thee better than any words of mine.

THIRTY YEARS UNTIL EMANCIPATION

I look back over thirty years, and call to mind all the circumstances of my journey to Philadelphia, in company with thyself and the excellent Dr. Thurston of Maine, even then, as we
thought, an old man, but still living, and true as ever to the
good cause. I recall the early gray morning when, with Samuel
J. May, our colleague on the Committee to prepare a Declaration of Sentiments for the Convention, I climbed to the small
"upper chamber" of a colored friend to hear thee read the first

Excerpted from "Letter: John G. Whittier to W.L. Garrison" by John Greenleaf Whittier, *William Lloyd Garrison, 1805–1879: The Story of His Life Told by His Children, Vol. IV
1861–1879* (New York: The Century Company, 1889).

draft of a paper which will live as long as our national history. I see the members of the Convention, solemnized by the responsibility, rise one by one, and solemnly affix their names to that stern pledge of fidelity to freedom. Of the signers, many have passed away from earth, a few have faltered and turned back, but I believe the majority still live to rejoice over the great triumph of truth and justice, and to devote what remains of time and strength to the cause to which they consecrated their youth and manhood thirty years ago.

For, while we may well thank God and congratulate one another on the prospect of the speedy emancipation of the slaves of the United States, we must not for a moment forget that, from this hour, new and mighty responsibilities devolve upon us to aid, direct, and educate these millions, left free, indeed, but bewildered, ignorant, naked, and foodless in the wild chaos of civil war. We have to undo the accumulated wrongs of two centuries; to remake the manhood that slavery has well-nigh unmade; to see to it that the long-oppressed colored man has a fair field for development and improvement; and to tread under our feet the last vestige of that hateful prejudice which has been the strongest external support of Southern slavery. We must lift ourselves at once to the true Christian altitude where all distinctions of black and white are overlooked in the heartfelt recognition of the brotherhood of man.

THANKING PROVIDENCE

I must not close this letter without confessing that I cannot be sufficiently thankful to the Divine Providence which, in a great measure through thy instrumentality, turned me so early away from what Roger Williams calls "the world's great trinity, pleasure, profit, and honor," to take side with the poor and oppressed. I am not insensible to literary reputation. I love, perhaps too well, the praise and good-will of my fellow-men; but I set a higher value on my name as appended to the Anti-Slavery Declaration of 1833 than on the title-page of any book. Looking over a life marked by many errors and shortcomings, I rejoice that I have been able to maintain the pledge of that signature; and that, in the long intervening years,

> 'My voice, though not the loudest, has been heard
> Wherever Freedom raised her cry of pain.'

Let me, through thee, extend a warm greeting to the friends, whether of our own or the new generation, who may assemble on the occasion of commemoration. There is work yet to be done which will task the best efforts of us all. For thyself, I need not say that the love and esteem of early boyhood have lost nothing by the test of time; and

I am, very cordially, thy friend,
JOHN G. WHITTIER.

CHAPTER 4

ABOLITIONIST VOICES

AMERICAN
SOCIAL
MOVEMENTS

The End of the *Liberator*

WILLIAM LLOYD GARRISON

William Lloyd Garrison's abolitionist newspaper, the *Liberator,* ran for nearly thirty-five years. After the Civil War and the passage of the Thirteenth Amendment, Garrison deemed his work as an abolitionist editor complete and the newspaper's purpose achieved. This is his valedictory letter to the public on December 29, 1865, in the final issue of the *Liberator.* In it he reflects on the newspaper's influence and reception, as well as his own future work now that slavery has ended. Garrison concludes with an emotional farewell to his readers.

"The last! the last! the last!
O, by that little word
How many thoughts are stirred
That sister of THE PAST!"

The present number of the *Liberator* is the completion of its thirty-fifth volume, and the termination of its existence.

Commencing my editorial career when only twenty years of age, I have followed it continuously till I have attained my sixtieth year—first, in connection with the *Free Press,* in Newburyport, in the spring of 1826; next, with the *National Philanthropist,* in Boston, in 1827; next, with the *Journal of the Times,* in Bennington, Vt., in 1828–9; next, with the *Genius of Universal Emancipation,* in Baltimore, in 1829–30; and, finally, with the *Liberator,* in Boston, from the 1st of January, 1831, to the 1st of January, 1866;—at the start, probably the youngest member of the editorial fraternity in the land, now, perhaps, the oldest, not in years, but in continuous service,—unless Mr. [William Cullen] Bryant, of the New York *Evening Post,* be an excep-

Excerpted from "Valedictory" by William Lloyd Garrison, *William Lloyd Garrison, 1805–1879: The Story of His Life Told by His Children, Vol. IV 1861–1879* (New York: The Century Company, 1889).

tion.

Whether I shall again be connected with the press, in a similar capacity, is quite problematical; but, at my period of life, I feel no prompting to start a new journal at my own risk, and with the certainty of struggling against wind and tide, as I have done in the past.

I began the publication of the *Liberator* without a subscriber, and I end it—it gives me unalloyed satisfaction to say—without a farthing as the pecuniary result of the patronage extended to it during thirty-five years of unremitted labors.

INFLUENCE OF THE *LIBERATOR*

From the immense change wrought in the national feeling and sentiment on the subject of slavery, the *Liberator* derived no advantage at any time in regard to its circulation. The original "disturber of the peace," nothing was left undone at the beginning, and up to the hour of the late rebellion, by Southern slaveholding villany on the one hand, and Northern pro-slavery malice on the other, to represent it as too vile a sheet to be countenanced by any claiming to be Christian or patriotic; and it always required rare moral courage or singular personal independence to be among its patrons. Never had a journal to look such opposition in the face—never was one so constantly belied and caricatured. If it had advocated all the crimes forbidden by the moral law of God and the statutes of the State, instead of vindicating the sacred claims of oppressed and bleeding humanity, it could not have been more vehemently denounced or more indignantly repudiated. To this day—such is the force of prejudice—there are multitudes who cannot be induced to read a single number of it, even on the score of curiosity, though their views on the slavery question are now precisely those which it has uniformly advocated. Yet no journal has been conducted with such fairness and impartiality; none has granted such freedom in its columns to its opponents; none has so scrupulously and uniformly presented all sides of every question discussed in its pages; none has so readily and exhaustively published, without note or comment, what its enemies have said to its disparagement and the vilification of its editor; none has vindicated primitive Christianity, in its spirit and purpose—"the higher law," in its supremacy over nations and governments as well as individual conscience—the Golden Rule, in its binding obligation upon all classes—the Declaration of Independence, with its self-evident truths—the rights of human nature, without distinction of race, complexion, or sex—more earnestly or more uncompromisingly; none has exerted a higher moral or more broadly reformatory influence upon those who have given it a careful perusal; and none has gone beyond it in asserting the Fatherhood of God and the brotherhood of man. All this may be claimed for it without egotism or presumption. It has ever been "a terror to evil-doers, and a praise

William Lloyd Garrison

to them that do well." It has excited the fierce hostility of all that is vile and demoniacal in the land, and won the affection and regard of the purest and noblest of the age. To me it has been unspeakably cheering, and the richest compensation for whatever of peril, suffering, and defamation I have been called to encounter, that one uniform testimony has been borne, by those who have had its weekly perusal, as to the elevating and quickening influence of the *Liberator* upon their character and lives; and the deep grief they are expressing in view of its discontinuance is overwhelmingly affecting to my feelings. Many of these date their subscriptions from the commencement of the paper, and they have allowed nothing in its columns to pass without a rigid scrutiny. They speak, therefore, experimentally, and "testify of that which they have seen and do know." Let them be assured that my regret in the separation which is to take place between us, in consequence of the discontinuance of the *Liberator*, is at least as poignant as their own; and let them feel, as I do, comforted by the thought that it relates only to the weekly method of communicating with each other, and not to the principles we have espoused in the past, or the hopes and aims we cherish as to the future.

Although the *Liberator* was designed to be, and has ever been, mainly devoted to the abolition of slavery, yet it has been instrumental in aiding the cause of reform in many of its most important aspects.

I have never consulted either the subscription-list of the paper or public sentiment in printing, or omitting to print, any article touching any matter whatever. Personally, I have never asked any one to become a subscriber, nor any one to contribute to its support, nor presented its claims for a better circulation in any lecture or speech, or at any one of the multitudinous anti-slavery gatherings in the land. Had I done so, no doubt its subscription-list might have been much enlarged.

THE FUTURE

In this connection, I must be permitted to express my surprise that I am gravely informed, in various quarters, that this is no time to retire from public labor; that though the chains of the captive have been broken, he is yet to be vindicated in regard to the full possession of equal civil and political rights; that the freedmen in every part of the South are subjected to many insults and outrages; that the old slaveholding spirit is showing itself in every available form; that there is imminent danger that, in the hurry of reconstruction and readmission to the Union, the late rebel States will be left free to work any amount of mischief; that there is manifestly a severe struggle yet to come with the Southern "powers of darkness," which will require the utmost vigilance and the most determined efforts on the part of the friends of impartial liberty—etc., etc., etc. Surely, it is not meant by all this that I am therefore bound to continue the publication of the *Liberator;* for that is a matter for me to determine, and no one else. As I commenced its publication without asking leave of any one, so I claim to be competent to decide when it may fitly close its career.

Again—it cannot be meant, by this presentation of the existing state of things at the South, either to impeach my intelligence, or to impute to me a lack of interest in behalf of that race for the liberation and elevation of which I have labored so many years! If, when they had no friends, and no hope of earthly redemption, I did not hesitate to make their cause my own, is it to be supposed that, with their yokes broken, and their friends and advocates multiplied indefinitely, I can be any the less disposed to stand by them to the last—to insist on the full measure of justice and equity being meted out to them— to retain in my breast a lively and permanent interest in all that relates to their present condition and future welfare?

I shall sound no trumpet and make no parade as to what I shall do for the future. After having gone through with such a struggle as has never been paralleled in duration in the life of any reformer, and for nearly forty years been the target at which all poisonous and deadly missiles have been hurled, and having seen our great national iniquity blotted out, and freedom "proclaimed throughout all the land to all the inhabitants thereof," and a thousand presses and pulpits supporting the claims of the colored population to fair treatment where not one could be found to do this in the early days of the anti-slavery conflict, I might—it seems to me—be permitted to take a little repose in my advanced years, if I desired to do so. But, as yet, I have neither asked nor wished to be relieved of any burdens or labors connected with the good old cause. I see a mighty work of enlightenment and regeneration yet to be accomplished at the South, and many cruel wrongs done to the freedmen which are yet to be redressed; and I neither counsel others to turn away from the field of conflict, under the delusion that no more remains to be done, nor contemplate such a course in my own case.

SLAVERY'S END

The object for which the *Liberator* was commenced—the extermination of chattel slavery—having been gloriously consummated, it seems to me specially appropriate to let its existence cover the historic period of the great struggle; leaving what remains to be done to complete the work of emancipation to other instrumentalities (of which I hope to avail myself), under new auspices, with more abundant means, and with millions instead of hundreds for allies.

Most happy am I to be no longer in conflict with the mass of my fellow-countrymen on the subject of slavery. For no man of any refinement or sensibility can be indifferent to the approbation of his fellow-men, if it be rightly earned. But to obtain it by going with the multitude to do evil—by pandering to despotic power or a corrupt public sentiment—is self-degradation and personal dishonor:

> "For more true joy Marcellus exiled feels
> Than Caesar with a Senate at his heels."

Better to be always in a minority of one with God—branded as madman, incendiary, fanatic, heretic, infidel—frowned upon by "the powers that be," and mobbed by the populace—or consigned ignominiously to the gallows, like him whose "soul is marching on," though his "body lies mouldering in the grave," or burnt to ashes at the stake like Wickliffe, or nailed to the cross like him who "gave himself for the world,"—in defence of the RIGHT, than like Herod, having the shouts of a multitude crying, "It is the voice of a god, and not of a man!"

Farewell, tried and faithful patrons! Farewell, generous benefactors, without whose voluntary but essential pecuniary contributions the *Liberator* must have long since been discontinued! Farewell, noble men and women who have wrought so long and so successfully, under God, to break every yoke! Hail, ye ransomed millions! Hail, year of jubilee! With a grateful heart and a fresh baptism of the soul, my last invocation shall be:

> "Spirit of Freedom, on!—
> Oh! pause not in thy flight
> Till every clime is won
> To worship in thy light:

Speed on thy glorious way,
And wake the sleeping lands!
Millions are watching for the ray,
And lift to thee their hands.
Still 'Onward!' be thy cry—
Thy banner on the blast;
And, like a tempest, as thou rushest by,
Despots shall shrink aghast.
On! till thy name is known
Throughout the peopled earth;
On! till thou reign'st alone,
Man's heritage by birth;
On! till from every vale, and where the mountains rise,
The beacon lights of Liberty shall kindle to the skies!"

A Former Slave Recounts His Escape

WILLIAM WELLS BROWN

William Wells Brown (1814?–1884), a fugitive slave and an abolitionist, had a black slave mother and a white slave-owning father. As a slave he served several masters, including slaveholder-turned-abolitionist Elijah P. Lovejoy. Brown was self-educated and involved in both the abolition and temperance movements. In this selection from his autobiography published in 1847, Brown recounts his escape from slavery. He tells us of a kind stranger who helped him, a Quaker named Wells Brown. It is from this man that the fugitive slave takes his name. The author also mentions his earliest acquaintance with the antislavery movement and how he became involved.

D uring the last night that I served in slavery, I did not close my eyes a single moment. When not thinking of the future, my mind dwelt on the past. The love of a dear mother, a dear sister, and three dear brothers, yet living, caused me to shed many tears. If I could only have been assured of their being dead, I should have felt satisfied; but I imagined I saw my dear mother in the cotton-field, followed by a merciless taskmaster, and no one to speak a consoling word to her! I beheld my dear sister in the hands of a slave-driver, and compelled to submit to his cruelty! None but one placed in such a situation can for a moment imagine the intense agony to which these reflections subjected me.

THE ESCAPE

At last the time for action arrived. The boat landed at a point which appeared to me the place of all others to start from. I

Excerpted from "Narrative of William W. Brown, a Fugitive Slave," by William Wells Brown, *Slave Narratives*, edited by William L. Andrews and Henry Louis Gates Jr. (New York: Literary Classics of America, 2000).

found that it would be impossible to carry anything with me, but what was upon my person. I had some provisions, and a single suit of clothes, about half worn. When the boat was discharging her cargo, and the passengers engaged carrying their baggage on and off shore, I improved the opportunity to convey myself with my little effects on land. Taking up a trunk, I went up the wharf, and was soon out of the crowd. I made directly for the woods, where I remained until night, knowing well that I could not travel, even in the State of Ohio, during the day, without danger of being arrested.

I had long since made up my mind that I would not trust myself in the hands of any man, white or colored. The slave is brought up to look upon every white man as an enemy to him and his race; and twenty-one years in slavery had taught me that there were traitors, even among colored people. After dark, I emerged from the woods into a narrow path, which led me into the main travelled road. But I knew not which way to go. I did not know North from South, East from West. I looked in vain for the North Star; a heavy cloud hid it from my view. I walked up and down the road until near midnight, when the clouds disappeared, and I welcomed the sight of my friend,—truly the slave's friend,—the North Star!

As soon as I saw it, I knew my course, and before daylight I travelled twenty or twenty-five miles. It being in the winter, I suffered intensely from the cold; being without an overcoat, and my other clothes rather thin for the season. I was provided with a tinder-box, so that I could make up a fire when necessary. And but for this, I should certainly have frozen to death; for I was determined not to go to any house for shelter. I knew of a man belonging to Gen. Ashly, of St. Louis, who had run away near Cincinnati, on the way to Washington, but had been caught and carried back into slavery; and I felt that a similar fate awaited me, should I be seen by any one. I travelled at night, and lay by during the day. . . .

My escape to a land of freedom now appeared certain, and the prospects of the future occupied a great part of my thoughts. What should be my occupation, was a subject of much anxiety to me; and the next thing what should be my name? . . . My old master, Dr. Young, had no children of his own, but had with him a nephew, the son of his brother, Benjamin Young. When this boy was brought to Doctor Young, his name being William, the same as mine, my mother was ordered to change mine to something else. This, at the time, I thought to be one of the most cruel acts that could be committed upon my rights; and I received several very severe whippings for telling people that my name was William, after orders were given to change it. Though young, I was old enough to place a high appreciation upon my name. It was decided, however, to call me "Sandford," and this name I was known by, not only upon my master's plantation, but up to the time that I made my escape. I was sold under the name of Sandford.

But as soon as the subject came to my mind, I resolved on adopting my old name of William, and let Sandford go by the board, for I always hated it. Not because there was anything peculiar in the name; but because it had been forced upon me. It is sometimes common at the south, for slaves to take the name of their masters. Some have a legitimate right to do so. But I always detested the idea of being called by the name of either of my masters. And as for my father, I would rather have adopted the name of "Friday," and been known as the servant of some Robinson Crusoe, than to have taken his name. So I was not only hunting for my liberty, but also hunting for a name; though I regarded the latter as of little consequence, if I could but gain the former. Travelling along the road, I would sometimes speak to myself, sounding my name over, by way of getting used to it, before I should arrive among civilized human beings. On the fifth or sixth day, it rained very fast, and it froze about as fast as it fell, so that my clothes were one glare of ice. I travelled on at night until I became so chilled and benumbed—the wind blowing into my face—that I found it impossible to go any further, and accordingly took shelter in a barn, where I was obliged to walk about to keep from freezing.

I have ever looked upon that night as the most eventful part of my escape from slavery. Nothing but the providence of

God, and that old barn, saved me from freezing to death. I received a very severe cold, which settled upon my lungs, and from time to time my feet had been frost-bitten, so that it was with difficulty I could walk. In this situation I travelled two days, when I found that I must seek shelter somewhere, or die.

The thought of death was nothing frightful to me, compared with that of being caught, and again carried back into slavery. Nothing but the prospect of enjoying liberty could have induced me to undergo such trials, for

"Behind I left the whips and chains,
Before me were sweet Freedom's plains!"

This, and this alone, cheered me onward. But I at last resolved to seek protection from the inclemency of the weather, and therefore I secured myself behind some logs and brush, intending to wait there until some one should pass by; for I thought it probable that I might see some colored person, or, if not, some one who was not a slaveholder; for I had an idea that I should know a slaveholder as far as I could see him.

A KIND STRANGER

The first person that passed was a man in a buggy-wagon. He looked too genteel for me to hail him. Very soon, another passed by on horseback. I attempted speaking to him, but fear made my voice fail me. As he passed, I left my hiding-place, and was approaching the road, when I observed an old man walking towards me, leading a white horse. He had on a broad-brimmed hat and a very long coat, and was evidently walking for exercise. As soon as I saw him, and observed his dress, I thought to myself, "You are the man that I have been looking for!" Nor was I mistaken. He was the very man!

On approaching me, he asked me, "if I was not a slave." I looked at him some time, and then asked him "if he knew of any one who would help me, as I was sick." He answered that he would; but again asked, if I was not a slave. I told him I was. He then said that I was in a very pro-slavery neighborhood, and if I would wait until he went home, he would get a covered wagon for me. I promised to remain. He mounted his horse, and was soon out of sight.

After he was gone, I meditated whether to wait or not; being apprehensive that he had gone for some one to arrest me. But I finally concluded to remain until he should return; removing some few rods to watch his movements. After a suspense of an hour and a half or more, he returned with a two horse covered-wagon, such as are usually seen under the shed of a Quaker meeting-house on Sundays and Thursdays; for the old man proved to be a Quaker of the George Fox stamp.

He took me to his house, but it was some time before I could be induced to enter it; not until the old lady came out, did I venture into the house. I thought I saw something in the old lady's cap that told me I was not only safe, but welcome, in her house. I was not, however, prepared to receive their hospitalities. The only fault I found with them was their being too kind. I had never had a white man to treat me as an equal, and the idea of a white lady waiting on me at the table was still worse! Though the table was loaded with the good things of this life, I could not eat. I thought if I could only be allowed the privilege of eating in the kitchen, I should be more than satisfied!

Finding that I could not eat, the old lady, who was a "Thompsonian," made me a cup of "composition," or "number six;" but it was so strong and hot, that I called it "*number seven!*" However, I soon found myself at home in this family. On different occasions, when telling these facts, I have been asked how I felt upon finding myself regarded as a man by a white family; especially just having run away from one. I cannot say that I have ever answered the question yet.

The fact that I was in all probability a freeman, sounded in my ears like a charm. I am satisfied that none but a slave could place such an appreciation upon liberty as I did at that time. I wanted to see mother and sister, that I might tell them "I was free!" I wanted to see my fellow slaves in St. Louis, and let them know that the chains were no longer upon my limbs. I wanted to see Captain Price, and let him learn from my own lips that I was no more a chattel, but a man! . . .

The fact that I was a freeman—could walk, talk, eat and sleep as a man, and no one to stand over me with the blood-clotted cowhide—all this made me feel that I was not myself.

The kind friend that had taken me in was named Wells Brown. He was a devoted friend of the slave; but was very old, and not in the enjoyment of good health. After being by the fire awhile, I found that my feet had been very much frozen. I was seized with a fever which threatened to confine me to my bed. But my Thompsonian friends soon raised me, treating me as kindly as if I had been one of their own children. I remained with them twelve or fifteen days, during which time they made me some clothing, and the old gentleman purchased me a pair of boots.

I found that I was about fifty or sixty miles from Dayton; in the State of Ohio, and between one and two hundred miles from Cleaveland, on Lake Erie, a place I was desirous of reaching on my way to Canada. This I know will sound strangely to the ears of people in foreign lands, but it is nevertheless true. An American citizen was fleeing from a Democratic, Republican, Christian government, to receive protection under the monarchy of Great Britain. While the people of the United States boast of their freedom, they at the same time keep three millions of their own citizens in chains; and while I am seated here in sight of Bunker Hill Monument, writing this narrative, I am a slave, and no law, not even in Massachusetts, can protect me from the hands of the slaveholder!

Before leaving this good Quaker friend, he inquired what my name was besides William. I told him that I had no other name. "Well," said he, "thee must have another name. Since thee has got out of slavery, thee has become a man, and men always have two names."

I told him that he was the first man to extend the hand of friendship to me, and I would give him the privilege of naming me.

"If I name thee," said he, "I shall call thee Wells Brown, after myself."

"But," said I, "I am not willing to lose my name of William.

As it was taken from me once against my will, I am not willing to part with it again upon any terms."

"Then," said he, "I will call thee William Wells Brown."

"So be it," said I; and I have been known by that name ever since I left the house of my first white friend, Wells Brown.

After giving me some little change, I again started for Canada. In four days I reached a public house, and went in to warm myself. I there learned that some fugitive slaves had just passed through the place. The men in the bar-room were talking about it, and I thought that it must have been myself they referred to, and I was therefore afraid to start, fearing they would seize me; but I finally mustered courage enough, and took my leave. As soon as I was out of sight, I went into the woods, and remained there until night, when I again regained the road, and travelled on until the next day.

Not having had any food for nearly two days, I was faint with hunger, and was in a dilemma what to do, as the little cash supplied me by my adopted father, and which had contributed to my comfort, was now all gone. I however concluded to go to a farm-house, and ask for something to eat. On approaching the door of the first one presenting itself, I knocked, and was soon met by a man who asked me what I wanted. I told him that I would like something to eat. He asked where I was from, and where I was going. I replied that I had come some way, and was going to Cleaveland.

After hesitating a moment or two, he told me that he could give me nothing to eat, adding, "that if I would work, I could get something to eat."

I felt bad, being thus refused something to sustain nature, but did not dare tell him that I was a slave.

Just as I was leaving the door, with a heavy heart, a woman, who proved to be the wife of this gentleman, came to the door, and asked her husband what I wanted? He did not seem inclined to inform her. She therefore asked me herself. I told her that I had asked for something to eat. After a few other questions, she told me to come in, and that she would give me something to eat.

I walked up to the door, but the husband remained in the passage, as if unwilling to let me enter.

She asked him two or three times to get out of the way, and let me in. But as he did not move, she pushed him on one side, bidding me walk in! I was never before so glad to see a woman push a man aside! Ever since that act, I have been in favor of "woman's rights!"

After giving me as much food as I could eat, she presented me with ten cents, all the money then at her disposal, accompanied with a note to a friend, a few miles further on the road. Thanking this angel of mercy from an overflowing heart, I pushed on my way, and in three days arrived at Cleaveland, Ohio.

Being an entire stranger in this place, it was difficult for me to find where to stop. I had no money, and the lake being frozen, I saw that I must remain until the opening of navigation, or go to Canada by way of Buffalo. But believing myself to be somewhat out of danger, I secured an engagement at the Mansion House, as a table waiter, in payment for my board. The proprietor, however, whose name was E.M. Segur, in a short time, hired me for twelve dollars per month; on which terms I remained until spring, when I found good employment on board a lake steamboat.

BECOMING AN ABOLITIONIST

I purchased some books, and at leisure moments perused them with considerable advantage to myself. While at Cleaveland, I saw, for the first time, an anti-slavery newspaper. It was the *"Genius of Universal Emancipation,"* published by Benjamin Lundy, and though I had no home, I subscribed for the paper. It was my great desire, being out of slavery myself, to do what I could for the emancipation of my brethren yet in chains, and while on Lake Erie, I found many opportunities of "helping their cause along."

It is well known, that a great number of fugitives make their escape to Canada, by way of Cleaveland; and while on the lake, I always made arrangement to carry them on the boat to Buffalo or Detroit, and thus effect their escape to the "promised land." The friends of the slave, knowing that I would transport them without charge, never failed to have a delegation when the boat arrived at Cleaveland. I have sometimes had four or five on board, at one time.

In the year 1842, I conveyed, from the first of May to the first of December, sixty-nine fugitives over Lake Erie to Canada. In 1843, I visited Malden, in Upper Canada, and counted seventeen, in that small village, who owed their escape to my humble efforts.

Soon after coming North, I subscribed for the Liberator, edited by that champion of freedom, William Lloyd Garrison. I labored a season to promote the temperance cause among the colored people, but for the last three years, have been pleading for the victims of American slavery.

On the Fugitive Slave Law

J.W. LOGUEN

The Rev. Jermain "Jarm" Wesley Loguen (1814–1872) was born into slavery in Tennessee and escaped to Canada. Later returning to the United States and gaining an education at the Oneida Institute in Whitesboro, New York, Loguen rose through the ranks of the African Methodist Episcopal Zion Church to become a bishop. He was a key member of the Underground Railroad in Syracuse and dedicated his autobiographical narrative to his railroad friends. In 1850 Congress passed the Fugitive Slave Law requiring that escaped slaves be returned to their masters regardless of whether they reached free soil in the North. Loguen attended a meeting in protest of the law held in the Syracuse City Hall. There, on October 4, 1850, he delivered this speech, which he recounts in his autobiography. In the address, Loguen is passionate about his God-given right to freedom. No one but the Almighty, the former slave tells the crowd, has a right to "own" another man's body and soul.

M r. Loguen was then called on, and took the stand. He looked over the great assembly, and said: He was a slave; he knew the dangers he was exposed to. He had made up his mind as to the course he was to take. On that score he needed no counsel, nor did the colored citizens generally. They had taken their stand—they would not be taken back to slavery. If to shoot down their assailants should forfeit their lives, such result was the least of the evil. They will have their liberties or die in their defence.

What is life to me if I am to be a slave in Tennessee? My neighbors! I have lived with you many years, and you know

Excerpted from *The Rev. J.W. Loguen as a Slave and as a Freeman: A Narrative of Real Life* (New York: Negro University Press, 1968).

me. My home is here, and my children were born here. I am bound to Syracuse by pecuniary interests, and social and family bonds. And do you think I can be taken away from you and from my wife and children, and be a slave in Tennessee? Has the President and his Secretary sent this enactment up here, to you, Mr. Chairman, to enforce on me in Syracuse?—and will you obey him? Did I think so meanly of you—did I suppose the people of Syracuse, strong as they are in numbers and love of liberty—or did I believe their love of liberty was so selfish, unmanly and unchristian—did I believe them so sunken and servile and degraded as to remain at their homes and labors, or, with none of that spirit which smites a tyrant down, to surround a United States Marshal to see me torn from my home and family, and hurled back to bondage—I say did I think so meanly of you, I could never come to live with you. Nor should I have stopped, on my return from Troy, twenty-four hours since, but to take my family and moveables to a neighborhood which would take fire, and arms, too, to resist the least attempt to execute this diabolical law among them. Some kind and good friends advise me to quit my country, and stay in Canada, until this tempest is passed. I doubt not the sincerity of such counsellors. But my conviction is strong, that their advice comes from a lack of knowledge of themselves and the case in hand. I believe that their own bosoms are charged to the brim with qualities that will smite to the earth the villains who may interfere to enslave any man in Syracuse. I apprehend the advice is suggested by the perturbation of the moment, and not by the tranquil spirit that rules above the storm, in the eternal home of truth and wisdom. Therefore have I hesitated to adopt this advice, at least until I have the opinion of this meeting. Those friends have not canvassed this subject. I have. They are called suddenly to look at it. I have looked at it steadily, calmly, resolutely, and at length defiantly, for a long time. I tell you the people of Syracuse and of the whole North must meet this tyranny and crush it by force, or be crushed by it.

This hellish enactment has precipitated the conclusion that

white men must live in dishonorable submission, and colored men be slaves, or they must give their physical as well as intellectual powers to the defence of human rights. The time has come to change the tones of submission into tones of defiance,—and to tell Mr. [President] Fillmore and Mr. [Secretary of State] Webster, if they propose to execute this measure upon us, to send on their blood-hounds. Mr. President, long ago I was beset by over prudent and good men and women to purchase my freedom. Nay, I was frequently importuned to consent that they purchase it, and present it as an evidence of their partiality to my person and character. Generous and kind as those friends were, my heart recoiled from the proposal. I owe my freedom to the God who made me, and who stirred me to claim it against all other beings in God's universe. I will not, nor will I consent, that any body else shall countenance the claims of a vulgar despot to my soul and body. Were I in chains, and did these kind people come to buy me out of prison, I would acknowledge the boon with inexpressible thankfulness. But I feel no chains, and am in no prison. I received my freedom from Heaven, and with it came the command to defend my title to it. I have long since resolved to do nothing and suffer nothing that can, in any way, imply that I am indebted to any power but the Almighty for my manhood and personality.

STAND WITH US IN RESISTANCE

Now, you are assembled here, the strength of this city is here to express their sense of this fugitive act, and to proclaim to the despots at Washington whether it shall be enforced here— whether you will permit the government to return me and other fugitives who have sought an asylum among you, to the Hell of slavery. The question is with you. If you will give us up, say so, and we will shake the dust from our feet and leave you. But we believe better things. We know you are taken by surprize. The immensity of this meeting testifies to the general consternation that has brought it together, necessarily, precipitately, to decide the most stirring question that can be presented, to wit, whether, the government having transgressed constitutional and natural limits, you will bravely resist its aggressions, and tell its soulless agents that no slave-holder shall make your city and county a hunting field for slaves.

"Whatever may be your decision, my ground is taken. I have declared it everywhere. It is known over the State and out of the State—over the line in the North, and over the line in the South. I don't respect this law—I don't fear it—I won't obey it! It outlaws me, and I outlaw it, and the men who attempt to enforce it on me. I place the governmental officials on the ground that they place me. I will not live a slave, and if force is employed to re-enslave me, I shall make preparations to meet the crisis as becomes a man. If you will stand by me—and I believe you will do it, for your freedom and honor are involved as well as mine—it requires no microscope to see that—I say if you will stand with us in resistance to this measure, you will be the saviours of your country. Your decision to-night in favor of resistance will give vent to the spirit of liberty, and it will break the bands of party, and shout for joy all over the North. Your example only is needed to be the type of popular action in Auburn, and Rochester, and Utica, and Buffalo, and all the West, and eventually in the Atlantic cities. Heaven knows that this act of noble daring will break out somewhere—and may God grant that Syracuse be the honored spot, whence it shall send an earthquake voice through the land!"

The words of a strong and brave man in the hour of peril fall like coals of fire on human hearts. The people knew Mr. Loguen and loved him. They knew he was a slave, and trembled for him. They listened with keen sympathy and breathless attention to his brief speech. They knew it was no occasion for Buncomb for any body, and least of all for him. His manliness and courage in a most trying crisis electrified them. He uncapped the volcano, and oppressed sympathy broke forth in a tempest of applause.

Reunion with a Former Master

FREDERICK DOUGLASS

Frederick Douglass (1817/18–1895) was a prominent abolitionist leader and one of the most important African American reformers of the nineteenth century. Born to a black slave mother and a white father, Douglass was a gifted orator who spoke openly about his escape from bondage. The positive reception to his eloquent anti-slavery speeches prompted him to write an autobiography, which has become a classic in American literature. This selection chronicles Douglass's meeting with his former master four decades after his escape. It is an encounter that is initially awkward. Ultimately, though, it is a meeting that seems to provide closure for both the former master and the former slave.

After a period of more than forty years, I visited and had an interview with [my former master] Captain Thomas Auld at St. Michaels, Talbot county, Maryland. . . . St. Michaels was at one time the place of my home and the scene of some of my saddest experiences of slave life, and . . . I left there, or rather was compelled to leave there, because it was believed that I had written passes for several slaves to enable them to escape from slavery, and that prominent slaveholders in that neighborhood had, for this alleged offense, threatened to shoot me on sight, and to prevent the execution of this threat my master had sent me to Baltimore.

THINKING ABOUT HIS RETURN

My return, therefore, in peace, to this place and among the same people, was strange enough in itself; but that I should, when there, be formally invited by Captain Thomas Auld, then over eighty years old, to come to the side of his dying bed, evidently with a view to a friendly talk over our past relations, was a fact still more strange, and one which, until its occurrence, I could never have thought possible. To me Captain Auld had sustained the relation of master—a relation which I had held in extremest abhorrence, and which for forty years I had denounced in all bitterness of spirit and fierceness of speech. He had struck down my personality, had subjected me to his will, made property of my body and soul, reduced me to a chattel, hired me out to a noted slave breaker to be worked like a beast and flogged into submission, taken my hard earnings, sent me to prison, offered me for sale, broken up my Sunday-school, forbidden me to teach my fellow-slaves to read on pain of nine and thirty lashes on my bare back and had, without any apparent disturbance of his conscience, sold my body to his brother Hugh and pocketed the price of my flesh and blood. I, on my part, had traveled through the length and breadth of this country and of England, holding up this conduct of his, in common with that of other slaveholders, to the reprobation of all men who would listen to my words. I had by my writings made his name and his deeds familiar to the world in four different languages, yet here we were, after four decades, once more face to face—he on his bed, aged and tremulous, drawing near the sunset of life, and I, his former slave, United States Marshal of the district of Columbia, holding his hand and in friendly conversation with him in a sort of final settlement of past differences preparatory to his stepping into his grave, where all distinctions are at an end, and where the great and the small, the slave and his master, are reduced to the same level. Had I been asked in the days of slavery to visit this man I should have regarded the invitation as one to put fetters on my ankles and handcuffs on my wrists. It would have been an invitation to the auction-block and the slave-whip. I had no business with this man under the old regime but to keep out of his way. But now that slavery was destroyed, and the slave and the master stood upon equal ground, I was not only willing to meet him, but was very glad to do so. The conditions were favorable for remembrance of all his good deeds, and generous extenuation of all his evil ones. He was to me no longer a slaveholder either in fact or in spirit, and I regarded him as I did myself, a victim of the circumstances of birth, education, law, and custom.

Frederick Douglass

Our courses had been determined for us, not by us. We had both been flung, by powers that did not ask our consent, upon a mighty current of life, which we could neither resist nor control. By this current he was a master, and I a slave; but now our lives were verging towards a point where differences disappear, where even the constancy of hate breaks down and where the clouds of pride, passion and selfishness vanish before the brightness of infinite light. At such a time, and in such a place, when a man is about closing his eyes on this world and ready to step into the eternal unknown, no word of reproach or bitterness should reach him or fall from his lips; and on this occasion there was to this rule no transgression on either side.

Explaining His Visit

As this visit to Capt. Auld has been made the subject of mirth by heartless triflers, and by serious-minded men regretted as a weakening of my life-long testimony against slavery, and as the report of it, published in the papers immediately after it occurred, was in some respects defective and colored, it may be proper to state exactly what was said and done at this interview.

It should in the first place be understood that I did not go to St. Michaels upon Capt. Auld's invitation, but upon that of my colored friend, Charles Caldwell; but when once there, Capt. Auld sent Mr. Green, a man in constant attendance upon him during his sickness, to tell me he would be very glad to see me, and wished me to accompany Green to his house, with which request I complied. On reaching the house I was met by Mr. Wm. H. Bruff, a son-in-law of Capt. Auld, and Mrs. Louisa Bruff, his daughter, and was conducted by them immediately to the bed-room of Capt. Auld. We addressed each other simultaneously, he calling me "Marshal Douglass," and I, as I had always called him, "Captain Auld." Hearing myself called by him "Marshal Douglass," I instantly broke up the formal nature of the meeting by saying, "not *Marshal,* but Frederick to you as formerly." We shook hands cordially, and in the act of doing so, he, having been long stricken with palsy, shed tears as men thus afflicted will do when excited by any deep emotion. The sight of him, the changes which time had wrought in him, his tremulous hands constantly in motion, and all the circumstances of his condition affected me deeply, and for a time choked my voice and made me speechless. We both, however, got the better of our feelings, and conversed freely about the past.

DOUGLASS AND AULD SPEAK

Though broken by age and palsy, the mind of Capt. Auld was remarkably clear and strong. After he had become composed I asked him what he thought of my conduct in running away and going to the north. He hesitated a moment as if to properly formulate his reply, and said: "Frederick, I always knew you were too smart to be a slave, and had I been in your place, I should have done as you did." I said, "Capt. Auld, I am glad to hear you say this. I did not run away from *you*, but from *slavery*; it was not that I loved Caesar less, but Rome more." I told him that I had made a mistake in my narrative, a copy of which I had sent him, in attributing to him ungrateful and cruel treatment of my grandmother; that I had done so on the supposition that in the division of the property of my old master, Mr. Aaron Anthony, my grandmother had fallen to him, and that he had left her in her old age, when she could be no longer of service to him, to pick up her living in solitude with none to help her, or, in other words, had turned her out to die like an old horse. "Ah!" he said, "that was a mistake, I never owned your grandmother; she in the division of the slaves was awarded to my brother-in-law, Andrew Anthony; but," he added quickly, "I brought her down here and took care of her as long as she lived." The fact is, that, after writing my narrative describing the condition of my grandmother, Capt. Auld's attention being thus called to it, he rescued her from her destitution. I told him that this mistake of mine was corrected as soon as I discovered it, and that I had at no time any wish to do him injustice; that I regarded both of us as victims of a system. "Oh, I never liked slavery," he said, "and I meant to emancipate all my slaves when they reached the age of twenty-five years." I told him I had always been curious to know how old I was and that it had been a serious trouble to me, not to know when was my birthday. He said he could not tell me that, but he thought I was born in February, 1818. This date made me one year younger than I had supposed myself. . . .

Before I left his bedside Captain Auld spoke with a cheerful confidence of the great change that awaited him, and felt himself about to depart in peace. Seeing his extreme weakness I did not protract my visit. The whole interview did not last more than twenty minutes, and we parted to meet no more. His death was soon after announced in the papers, and the fact that he had once owned me as a slave was cited as rendering that event noteworthy.

Slavery and the Evils of War

MONCURE DANIEL CONWAY

Moncure Daniel Conway (1832–1907) was an abolitionist and Unitarian minister born in Virginia. He was an author of over seventy books. Conway believed in a more tempered abolitionism, one that could achieve its ends without bloodshed. Feeling that abolitionists in America were too militant, he lobbied for the cause abroad. Conway believed he could benefit the movement through contacts with influential members of society in Great Britain and through sermons and correspondence. In these sections of his autobiography, Conway shares his explanation for going to London on his crusade for peaceful abolition. He also gives his opinions of such prominent figures as Abraham Lincoln and John Brown, indicating how and why both trod dangerous and often ruinous paths in the name of ending oppression. Conway struggles with a desire for emancipation but repulsion from war, even if it will end slavery.

The cause in which I was interested was liberty; I would not have advocated bloodshed even for emancipation, though anxious since war had come that it should be the means of destroying slavery. I would have considered the Union apart from emancipation not worth one man's blood. I was thus too different from other Americans—even from my antislavery colleagues—to be directly useful in the republican campaign. I had no faith that war could achieve any permanent benefit to white, or black, or to any nation, while the President and the people recognized only the military method of pacification and emancipation. There was thus no place for me in militant America.

Excerpted from *Autobiography: Memories and Experiences of Moncure Daniel Conway in Two Volumes, Volume II*, by Moncure Daniel Conway (Cambridge, MA: The Riverside Press, 1904).

London had cordially offered me what my native country had not—a field for the exercise of the ministry for which my strange pilgrimage from slaveholding Virginia and Methodism to freedom and rationalism had trained me. So . . . reason bade me stay where I was wanted for tasks to which I felt that I could bring some competency. So it was that, having gone to England for a few months, I remained more than thirty years. . . .

CONWAY ON LINCOLN

Abraham Lincoln, ten years before his election to the presidency, was for a short time in Congress. His brief career there was marked by one proposal and one utterance. The proposal was that there should be added to a measure for abolishing slavery in the District of Columbia a provision for the rendition to their owners of slaves escaping into the District, which otherwise might be crowded with negroes seeking asylum there. He was the same man when he said to our deputation: "Suppose I should put in the South these antislavery generals and governors; what could they do with the slaves that would come to them?"

His notable utterance in Congress was his description of military glory as "That rainbow that rises in showers of blood—that serpent eye that charms but to destroy."

When he became President, Lincoln wrote privately to a Quaker: "Your people have had and are having very great trials on principles and faith. Opposed to both war and oppression, they can only practically oppose oppression by war."

But the very State that fired on Fort Sumter had candidly indicated to the new President, before that event, how both secession and oppression could be vanquished without war. Representative Ashmore of South Carolina said in Congress: "The South can sustain more men in the field than the North. Her four millions of slaves alone will enable her to support an army of half a million."

President Lincoln had only to use the war power thrust into his hand by slavery to proclaim those four millions free; the boasted commissariat of the Southern army would have existed no longer when every Northern camp was the slave's asylum; slavery, the *teterrima causa,* would have needed every Southern white to guard it. Repeatedly was this urged on the President, along with the fact that every loyalist's slave might be paid for with a month's cost of war.

In his message to Congress, December, 1863, the President said: "Of those who were slaves at the beginning of the rebellion full 100,000 are now in the United States military service, about half of which number actually bear arms in the ranks,—thus giving the double advantage of *taking so much labor from the insurgent cause,"* etc. The President had precisely the same right to take 4,000,000 of black labourers from the insurgent cause as 100,000, with the million-fold "advantage"of preventing the war altogether. After 300,000 soldiers had been slaughtered, thousands of families draped in mourning, commerce by land and sea paralyzed, hostility towards England and France engendered, thousands of fugitive slaves thrust back into slavery, and billions of money wasted, the President came no nearer meeting oppression with liberty than to put his livery on 100,000 negroes, set them to cut the throats of their former masters, and sow new seeds of race hatred.

The evils of slavery as a domestic institution were mere pimples compared with the evils of war. The greater evils of slavery were that it kept the country generally in a state of chronic war, now and then breaking out into acute eruptions, such as the murderous robbery of Mexico and the outrages on Kansas. When secession seemed to be slavery withdrawing from its aggressiveness, antislavery men welcomed it; when the firing on Fort Sumter seemed to be another war on liberty, we felt that liberty had to be defended. Even when it was plain that the war was being waged by the President, not for liberty, but solely for the Union, the probabilities that it would somehow eradicate the root of discord from the nation, rendered it necessary to support the Northern side, there being no prospect of stopping the war. But slavery originated in war, and in 1864 it became clear that the war which we were trying to turn against slavery was protecting it. Habeas corpus was suspended; free speech suppressed; men were drafted and torn from their families by violence to fight the South; slaves were armed and put on much less than the pay given white soldiers; and in 1864 the first attempt to reconstruct a rebel State—Louisiana—was by forcing the loyal negroes to work for their old masters (all rebels), albeit for paltry wages. The disloyal whites were to have suffrage, but not the blacks. The prospect was that in all the reconstructed States slavery was to return as serfdom. . . .

John Brown and the Evils of War

On December 2, 1863, a public meeting convened by the Emancipation Society was held in the Whittington Club Hall to commemorate the fourth anniversary of the execution of John Brown. The chair was taken by William Malleson, who in his opening speech related the mythical story that on his way to the scaffold Brown stopped and gave a kiss to a little negro girl. The meeting had been convened to listen to an address from myself, and this was published by the society. In it I said, "Brown's plan was the best his eye could scan; but it would only have done in Virginia what he had already done in Kansas,— free a few slaves. But God's plan was a different one from that. It included the placing of the angel Justice side by side with the fiend Oppression, that the world should see them ere the foot of the one was planted on the neck of the other."

I am now certain that no god had anything to do with the affair except the phantasmal god of war worshipped by Brown, and that the biblical captain who revived that deified wrath inflicted on America sequels of slavery worse than the disease.

CHRONOLOGY

1619
Twenty Africans are sold to settlers in Virginia.

1688
In Germantown, Pennsylvania, the Society of Friends (Quakers) drafts the earliest American antislavery document.

1700
The first antislavery tract, *The Selling of Joseph* by Samuel Sewall, is published and distributed in the colonies.

1764
In his pamphlet *The Rights of the British Colonies Asserted and Proved,* James Otis Jr. suggests that natural law means that all people, both blacks and whites, are born free and equal.

1787
The Northwest Ordinance, drafted by Thomas Jefferson, is passed; it bans slavery in the western territory (acquired from England during the Revolutionary War) north of the Ohio River.

1793
The first fugitive slave law is passed.

1794
The American Convention, composed of delegates from local and state antislavery societies, meets for the first time in Philadelphia to promote gradual abolition.

1807
A law is passed forbidding the importation of slaves into the United States as of January 1, 1808.

1816
The American Colonization Society is formed; the society advocates the returning of free blacks to Africa.

1820
The Missouri Compromise is passed; it admits into the Union one slave state (Missouri) and one free state (Maine); it also decrees that new states north of the 36°30' line will be free and new states south of that latitude will be slave states.

1822
Denmark Vesey, a free black, is betrayed by a black informant and is executed after his five-year effort to organize a slave rebellion in Charleston, South Carolina.

1831
The Nat Turner slave revolt takes place in Virginia; William Lloyd Garrison launches the *Liberator,* an abolitionist newspaper.

1833
Lydia Maria Child publishes *An Appeal in Favor of That Class of Americans Called Africans;* the American Anti-Slavery Society is founded; the British Empire abolishes slavery.

1836
A "gag rule" is passed in the House of Representatives.

1837
The murder of abolitionist editor Elijah Lovejoy takes place in Alton, Illinois.

1839
A slave revolt occurs onboard the *Amistad;* the African rebels are eventually freed after John Quincy Adams argues on their behalf before the Supreme Court.

1840

The American Anti-Slavery Society splits; Garrison remains part of it until its dissolution in 1870; Arthur and Lewis Tappan form the American and Foreign Anti-Slavery Society; the Liberty Party, the first antislavery political party, is formed and lasts until the organization of the Free Soil Party in 1848.

1844

The congressional "gag rule" is repealed.

1847

William Wells Brown's autobiography, *Narrative of William W. Brown, a Fugitive Slave,* is published.

1848

The Free Soil Party, a coalition of Northern Whigs, Northern Democrats, and Liberty abolitionists, is formed.

1849

Harriet Tubman escapes from slavery and becomes a key member of the Underground Railroad.

1850

The Compromise of 1850 is passed; under it, California is admitted as a free state, New Mexico and Utah are afforded popular sovereignty (the power to decide the slavery question on their own), and the slave trade is abolished in Washington, D.C.; in addition, a tougher Fugitive Slave Law is passed, penalizing anyone who interferes with the pursuit and capture of fugitive slaves.

1852

Harriet Beecher Stowe's antislavery novel, *Uncle Tom's Cabin,* is published.

1854

The Republican Party is founded; the Kansas-Nebraska Act, allowing those territories to decide the slavery question by popular sovereignty, is passed; this legislation nullifies the Missouri Compromise.

1857

In *Dred Scott v. Sandford,* the Supreme Court protects the extension of slavery and declares that blacks are not citizens.

1859

John Brown stages a raid on Harpers Ferry, Virginia; his plan to start an armed slave rebellion fails, and Brown is hanged for his treasonous act.

1860

Abraham Lincoln is elected president; South Carolina secedes from the Union.

1861

The Civil War begins.

1862

Lincoln issues the Emancipation Proclamation, which frees slaves in the seceded states and makes emancipation a war aim.

1863

The Emancipation Proclamation takes effect; it has little immediate effect since most slaves are still behind Southern battle lines.

1865

The Civil War ends; the Thirteenth Amendment, which legally ends slavery, is ratified; publication of the *Liberator* comes to an end.

FOR FURTHER RESEARCH

Herbert Aptheker, *Abolitionism: A Revolutionary Movement.* Boston: Twayne, 1989.

Gilbert Hobbs Barnes, *The Antislavery Impulse, 1830–1844.* New York: Harcourt, Brace, and World, 1964.

R.J.M. Blackett, *Building an Antislavery Wall: Black Americans in the Atlantic Antislavery Movement, 1830–1860.* Baton Rouge: Louisiana State University Press, 1983.

William Wells Brown, *Narrative of William W. Brown, a Fugitive Slave,* in *Slave Narratives,* comps. William L. Andrews and Henry Louis Gates Jr. New York: Literary Classics of America, 2000.

Henrietta Buckmaster, *Flight to Freedom: The Story of the Underground Railroad.* New York: Dell, 1972.

Roger Burns, ed., *Am I Not a Man and a Brother: The Antislavery Crusade of Revolutionary America.* New York: Chelsea House, 1977.

Lydia Maria Child, *An Appeal in Favor of That Class of Americans Called Africans.* Ed. Carolyn Karcher. Amherst: University of Massachusetts Press, 1996.

Moncure Daniel Conway, *Autobiography: Memories and Experiences of Moncure Daniel Conway in Two Volumes.* Cambridge, MA: Riverside, 1904.

David Brion Davis, *The Problem of Slavery in the Age of Revolution, 1770–1823.* Ithaca, NY: Cornell University Press, 1975.

Merton L. Dillon, *The Abolitionists: The Growth of a Dissenting Minority.* De Kalb: Northern Illinois University Press, 1974.

Frederick Douglass, *The Narrative and Selected Writings.* Ed. Michael Meyer. New York: Modern Library, 1984.

Thomas E. Drake, *Quakers and Slavery in America*. New Haven, CT: Yale University Press, 1950.

Martin Duberman, ed., *The Antislavery Vanguard: New Essays on the Abolitionists*. Princeton, NJ: Princeton University Press, 1965.

W.E.B. Du Bois, *John Brown*. Millwood, NY: Kraus-Thomson Organization Limited, 1973.

James D. Essig, *The Bonds of Wickedness: American Evangelicals Against Slavery, 1770–1808*. Philadelphia: Temple University Press, 1982.

Louis Filler, ed., *Abolition and Social Justice in the Era of Reform*. New York: Harper and Row, 1972.

Eric Foner, *The Story of American Freedom*. New York: W.W. Norton, 1998.

William Freehling, *Road to Disunion*. New York: Oxford University Press, 1990.

Wendell Phillips Garrison and Francis Jackson Garrison, *William Lloyd Garrison, 1805–1879: Story of His Life as Told by His Children*. Vol. 4. *1861–1879*. New York: Century, 1889.

Stanley Harrold, *American Abolitionists*. Harlow, England: Pearson Education Limited, 2001.

Michael Holt, *The Political Crisis of the 1850s*. New York: Wiley, 1978.

Aileen S. Kraditor, *Means and Ends in American Abolitionism: Garrison and His Critics on Strategy and Tactics, 1834–1850*. New York: Pantheon Books, 1969.

Bruce Levine, *Half Slave and Half Free: The Roots of the Civil War*. New York: Hill and Wang, 1992.

J.W. Loguen, *The Rev. J.W. Loguen as a Slave and as a Freeman: A Narrative of Real Life*. New York: Negro Universities Press, 1968.

Donald C. Mathews, ed., *Agitation for Freedom: The Abolitionist Movement*. New York: John Wiley and Sons, 1972.

Henry Mayer, *All on Fire: William Lloyd Garrison and the Abolition of Slavery.* New York: St. Martin's, 1998.

John R. McKivigan and Mitchell Snay, eds., *Religion and the Antebellum Debate over Slavery*. Athens: University of Georgia Press, 1998.

James M. McPherson, *The Abolitionist Legacy: From Reconstruction to the NAACP.* 2nd ed. Princeton, NJ: Princeton University Press, 1995.

Edmund Morgan, *American Slavery, American Freedom*. New York: W.W. Norton, 1975.

James Oakes, *Slavery and Freedom: An Interpretation of the Old South*. New York: Knopf, 1990.

Jane H. Pease and William H. Pease, *Bound with Them in Chains: A Biographical History of the Antislavery Movement.* Westport, CT: Greenwood, 1972.

David M. Potter, *The Impending Crisis, 1848–1861.* New York: Harper and Row, 1976.

Benjamin Quarles, *Black Abolitionists*. 1969. Reprint, New York: Oxford University Press, 1977.

Louis Ruchames, ed., *The Abolitionists: A Collection of Their Writings*. New York: G.P. Putnam's Sons, 1963.

Richard Sewell, *Ballots for Freedom: Anti-Slavery Politics, 1837–1861*. New York: Oxford University Press, 1976.

Henry H. Simms, *A Decade of Sectional Controversy: 1851–1861.* Westport, CT: Greenwood, 1978.

Ronald G. Walters, *The Antislavery Appeal: American Abolitionism After 1830*. Baltimore: Johns Hopkins University Press, 1976.

INDEX

churches' views on, 31, 73–74
disregarded in the
    Declaration of
    Independence, 39–40
economic dependence on,
    26–27, 52–54
European, 11–12
evils of, 40–41, 83–84
    vs. evils of war, 176–77
example of, 99
vs. freed labor
    argument for, 99–100
    economic benefits of, 96–97
    motives for laboring and,
    97–98
history of American, 12–13
North/South political
    tensions over, 117–21,
    128–30
Revolution's contradictory
    impact on, 32–33
rights and laws on, 101
territorial expansion of,
    106–107
Virginia debate on, 102–103
see also antislavery movement;
    emancipation; slaves
slaves
as abolitionist activists, 17
deported to America, 12
escape by, 156–61
freed
    in the armed forces, 135,
    138–39, 175–76
    becoming abolitionists,
    163–64
    citizenship for, 141
    education for, 48–49
    employment for, 163
    land distribution for, 139,
    141

moving to the North, 53
new names for, 161–62
problems confronting, 23
removing from America,
    46–47, 134–35
reunion with former
    master, 169–73
speech on Fugitive Slave
    Law by, 165–68
William Lloyd Garrison on,
    152–53
Liberty Party's aid to, 111–12
petitioning for freedom,
    29–30
population, 15, 17, 33
unrest of, 108
see also slavery
slave trade
    British debate on, 61
    Constitution on, 31–32
    legislation ending, 49–50
Smith, Gerrit, 110, 126
Snay, Mitchell, 72
societies, 13
    American Convention, 15
    on evils of slavery, 40–41
    increasing aggressiveness of,
    105–106
    intentions of, 34–35
    number of, 18, 63
    plan for emancipation by,
    41–44
    on reasons for abolition,
    36–37
    recommendations by, 37–38
    see also abolitionists; National
    Anti-Slavery Society
Society for the Relief of Free
    Negroes Unlawfully Held in
    Bondage, 13
Society of Friends. See